God's Plan
for Your Life

For a Closer Walk with Him

GARY M. DANNER

Trilogy Christian Publishers
A Wholly Owned Subsidary of Trinity Broadcasting Network
2442 Michelle Drive
Tustin, CA 92780

Dates have been taken from *The Annals of the World* by James Ussher.

Definitions of Greek and Hebrew words have been taken form *Strong's Exhaustive Concordance of the Bible* by James Strong.

Scriptures are from the King James Version of the Bible except for a few from the Amplified for emphasis.

Definitions of Christian concepts have been taken from *Webster Dictionary*.

For information, address Trilogy Christian Publishing
Rights Department, 2442 Michelle Drive, Tustin, Ca 92780.
Trilogy Christian Publishing/ TBN and colophon are trademarks of Trinity Broadcasting Network.

For information about special discounts for bulk purchases, please contact Trilogy Christian Publishing.

Manufactured in the United States of America

10 9 8 7 6 5 4 3 2 1

Library of Congress Cataloging-in-Publication Data is available.

ISBN 978-1-64773-837-2 (Print Book)
ISBN 978-1-64773-838-9 (ebook)

Jesus described and demonstrated a new dimension of reality that mankind hasn't comprehended, and He has given us the ability to move from a worldly dimension to a heavenly one through understanding His message.

Before we can understand the plans that God has for each of our lives to prosper us and maximize our peace, love, joy, and productivity, we need to look at who God is, who we are, and the reality of the world we live in.

Contents

Foreword

This book is the story of my walk toward God and ties together some of the major themes and mysteries of the Bible that relate to the Christian life. It may help us understand who God is, who we are, and what God's plans are for planet Earth and each of us. It affords a different perspective of biblical truth and is intended to expand our understanding of reality by looking at what God says is true. Jesus said He came that we could have life and have it more abundantly. Eternal life will definitely do that, but there may be more that can be experienced now. It is written that as a man thinks, so is he, and for lack of knowledge, a person perishes. Believing the truth will set us free here and now and will lead to eternal life when we pass over. This book is comprised of many years of notes and studies I have collected while attending and teaching Bible studies at several different denominations in several different states and in Spain. The book ends with a look at prophecy that has come to pass and prophecy of future events.

Acknowledgments

A special thank-you to those who helped me with this book: Claudette Stroble and Ronnie Goodin, for comments and editing; and Jim Kline, for legal counsel.

CHAPTER 1

Who Is God?

Forming a Relationship with God

The Bible is the story of God introducing Himself to mankind and revealing His plans for earth and mankind. He provides mankind a way to abundant eternal life with Him in heaven. His plan may resemble a wedding ceremony between God and mankind, where He introduces Himself, pursues us, forms a relationship with us, proposes marriage to us, gives us an engagement ring (the Holy Spirit), and goes away to prepare a place for us at His Father's house with a promise to return and take us home.

The first requirement needed to start any relationship is exchanging names. We introduce ourselves to each other. God introduced Himself to Moses in Exodus 3:14. He called himself "I Am Who I Am." In Hebrew, it is represented as four letters, YHWH, and is pronounced "Jehovah" or "Yahweh." This name was only a starting point, and as time went on, God started revealing more about Himself through different names. Through these different names we see God's nature. As time went on, God started revealing His many titles and attributes, making promises through contracts or covenants with mankind. Through Jesus many more attributes of God were revealed.

Through miracles, Jesus demonstrated power over time, space, and matter. He changed water into a vintage wine, raised the dead, healed people from a distance, and walked on water.

The Names of God in the Old Testament

1. El—the strong one (singular) (2 Sam. 22:33)
2. El Elyon—the most-high God (Gen. 14:18–22)
3. El Olam—the everlasting God (Gen. 21:33)
4. El Shaddai—the almighty one (Gen. 17:1) (almighty nurturer)
5. Elohim—the all-powerful one (plural) (Gen. 1:1)
6. Jehovah—the self-existent one (I Am) (Exod. 3:14)
7. Jehovah-Elohim—Lord God, Creator (Gen. 2:4)
8. Jehovah-Jireh—Jehovah will provide (Gen. 22:13–14)
9. Jehovah-Nissi—Jehovah is my victory (Exod. 17:15)
10. Jehovah-Raah—Jehovah is my Shepherd (Ps. 23:1)
11. Jehovah-Rapha—Jehovah that Heals (Exod. 15:25–26)
12. Jehovah-Saboath—Lord of hosts (Ps. 46:7, 11)
13. Jehovah-Shalom—Jehovah is peace (Judg. 6:24)
14. Jehovah-Shammah—Jehovah is there (Ezek. 48:35)
15. Jehovah Tsid Kenu—Jehovah our righteousness (Jer. 33:16)

The First Name

The first name God calls himself is Elohim, the all-powerful one (plural) (Gen. 1:1). This name refers to God as being an all-powerful creator of both heaven and earth.

Most-High God

"Most high," or "most-high God" (in Hebrew, El Elyon). *Elyon* means simply "highest."

The first revelation of this name (Gen. 14:8) indicates its distinctive meanings. When Abram returned from his victory over the confederated kings (Gen. 14:1–17), he was met by Melchizedek, king of Salem, the "priest of the most-high God" (El Elyon), who blessed Abram in the name of El Elyon, "possessor of heaven and earth." This revelation produced a remarkable impression upon the patriarch. Not only did he at once give Melchizedek tithes of all the spoil of the battle, but also, when the king of Sodom offered other spoils to Abram, his answer was, "I have lift up mine hand unto the Lord [Jehovah], the most high God [El Elyon], the possessor of heaven and earth, that I will not take a thread or even a shoe latchet" etc. (Gen. 14:18–23).

Appropriately, to this Gentile knowledge of God by His name "Most High," we read that the Most High divided to the nations (i.e., Gentiles) their inheritance when He separated the sons of Adam (Deut. 32:8). As He was the possessor of heaven and earth, it was the prerogative of the Most High to distribute the earth among the nations according to whatever principle He chose. That principle is declared in Daniel, the book of Gentile prophecy (Dan. 3:26; 4:17, 24, 25, 32–35; 5:18, 21). The Gentile high priest's name Melchizedek means "king of righteousness" (Heb. 7:2). Jesus is priest, not after the order of Arron, but after the order of Melchizedek.

As "possessor of heaven and earth," the most-high God has and exercises authority in both spheres of heaven and earth:

    a)   The heavenly authority of El Elyon (Dan. 4:35, 37; Isa. 14:13–14; Matt. 28:18)

    b)   The earthly authority of El Elyon (Deut. 32:8; Ps. 9:2–5, 21:7, 47:2–4; 56:2–3; 82:6, 8; 83:16–18; 91:9–12; 2 Sam. 22:14, 15; Dan. 5:18)

LORD (all capitals) in the King James Version of the Bible is from the Hebrew word written YHWH and is pronounced "Jehovah" or "Yahweh." Since there are no vowels in Hebrew, it can be pronounced either way. It was a holy word not to be spoken and thus is called the ineffable name of God. The shortened version of YHWH is Ja, pronounced Ya, like when we sing "Ha-le-lu-ya."

The primary meaning of the name LORD (Jehovah) is the "self-existent one." Literally (as in Exod. 3:14), "He that is who He is, therefore the eternal I Am."

But Havah, from which Jehovah, or Yahweh, is formed, signifies also "to become," that is, to become known, thus pointing to a continuous and increasing self-revelation. Combining these meanings of Havah, we arrive at the meaning of the name Jehovah. He is "the self-existent one who reveals Himself." The name is, in itself, an advance upon the name "God" (El, Elah, Elohim), which suggests certain attributes of deity, such as strength, rather than His essential being.

It is significant that the first appearance of the name Jehovah in Scripture follows the fall of man. It was God (Elohim) who said, "Let us make man in our image" (Gen. 1:26), but after man sins in Genesis chapter 2, it is the Lord God (Jehovah-Elohim) who acts.

Jehovah is distinctly the redemption name of deity. When sin entered and redemption became necessary, it was Jehovah-Elohim who sought the sinning ones (Gen. 3:9–13) and clothed them with "coats of skins" (Gen. 3:21), a beautiful type of righteousness provided by the Lord God through blood sacrifice (Rom. 3:21–22). The first distinct revelation of Himself by His name Jehovah was in connection with the redemption of the covenant people out of Egypt (Exod. 3:13–17). With Him as Redeemer, emphasis is laid upon those attributes of Jehovah that the sin and salvation of man bring into effect. These are thus:

a) His holiness (Lev. 11:44–45, 19:1–2, 20:26; Hab. 1:12–13).

b) His hatred and judgment of sin (Deut. 32:35–42; Gen. 6:5–7; Ps. 11:4–6, 66:18; Exod. 34:6–7).

c) His love for and redemption of sinners (Gen. 3:21, 8:20–21; Exod. 12:12–13; Lev. 16:2–3; Isa. 53:5–6, 10). Salvation by Jehovah apart from blood sacrifice is unknown to Scripture. That's why Cain's sacrifice from his garden was unacceptable and why the fig leaves that covered Adam and Eve in the garden were unacceptable. God replaced the fig leaves with bloody animal skins that covered both their physical and spiritual bodies.

In His redemptive relation to man, Jehovah has seven compound names that reveal Him as meeting every need of man from his lost state to the end. These compound names are thus:

1.   Jehovah-jireh, "the Lord will provide" (Gen. 22:13–14)—i.e., will provide a sacrifice.
2.   Jehovah-rapha, "the Lord that heals" (Exod. 15:26). That this refers to physical healing, the context shows, but the deeper healing of soul malady is implied.
3.   Jehovah-nissi, "the Lord our banner" (Exod. 17:8–15). The name is interpreted by the context. The enemy was Amalek, a type of the flesh, and the conflict that day stands for the conflict of the war of the Spirit against the flesh (Gal. 5:17). Victory was wholly due to divine help.
4.   Jehovah-shalom, "the Lord our peace," or "the Lord send peace" (Judg. 6:24). Almost the whole ministry of Jehovah finds expression and illustration in that chapter. Jehovah hates and judges sin (Gen. 2:1–5). Jehovah loves and saves sinners (Gen. 2:7–18), but only through sacrifice (Gen. 2:19–21; see also Rom. 5:1, Eph. 2:14, Col. 1:20).
5.   Jehovah-ra-ah, "the Lord my shepherd" (Ps. 23). In Psalm 22 Jehovah makes peace by the blood of the cross; in Psalm 23, Jehovah is shepherding His own who are in the world.
6.   Jehovah-tsidkenu, "the Lord our righteousness" (Jer. 23:6). This name of Jehovah occurs in a prophecy concerning the future restoration and conversion of Israel. Then Israel will hail him as Jehovah-tsidkenu, "the Lord our righteousness."

7. Jehovah-shammah, "the Lord is present" (Ezek. 48:35). This name signifies Jehovah's abiding presence with His people (Exod. 33:14–15; 1 Chron. 16:27, 33; Ps. 16:11, 97:5; Matt. 28:20; Heb. 13:5).

The word *Lord* (not all capitals) in the King James Version of the Bible is from the Hebrew word written *Adonai*. The primary meaning of *Adon, Adonai*, is "master," and it is applied in the Old Testament scriptures both to deity and to men.

Lord (Jehovah) is also the distinctive name of deity used when in covenant with Israel (Exod. 19:3, 20:1–2; Jer. 31:31–34).

Lord God (Hebrew Jehovah-Elohim) is the first of the compound names of deity. Lord God is used distinctly as Creator (Gen. 2:7–15), as governing the earthly relationships of man (Gen. 2:18–24, 3:16–19, 3:22–24) and as redeeming man (Gen. 3:8–15, 21).

The Names of Holy Spirit

The Hebrews knew of a coming Redeemer or Messiah, and they saw the work and power of the Holy Spirit, especially in war, but were not aware of God's plans for saving the world. The names and symbols of the Holy Spirit are found in the New Testament:

- Dove (seen at Jesus's baptism) (Matt. 3:16; Ps. 68:13)
- Holy Spirit (John 14:26)

- Spirit of wisdom (Exod. 28:3; Deut. 34:9; Eph. 1:17)
- Spirit of CHRIST (1 Pet. 1:11)
- Comforter (John 14:16; 14:26)
- Intercessor (one who stands in for a person)

> *Likewise the Spirit also helpeth our infir-*
> *mities: for we know not what we should*
> *pray for as we ought: but the Spirit itself*
> *maketh intercession for us with groanings*
> *which cannot be uttered.* *27 And he that*
> *searcheth the hearts knoweth what is the*
> *mind of the Spirit, because he maketh*
> *intercession for the saints according to the*
> *will of God. (Rom. 8:26–27 KJV)*

Paraclete (Greek: παράκλητος; Latin: paracletus) means advocate or helper. In Christianity, the term *paraclete* most commonly refers to the Holy Spirit.

- Presence of God (can be felt, but not seen) (Gen. 3:8; Ps. 68:2,8)
- Spirit of God (Gen. 1:2, 41:38; Exod. 35:31)
- Spirit of truth (John 15:13, 26)
- Breath of God (Gen. 2:7; Job 33:4; Ezek. 37:9)

Holy Spirit Has Attributes of a Person

- The Spirit consciously moves (Gen. 1:2).
- He instructs and teaches (Neh. 9:20; John 14:26).
- Some hide from His presence (Ps. 139:7).
- He has emotion, is grieved or vexed (Isa. 63:10).

- He has presence, personally (Isa. 63:11).
- He gives people rest as did Jesus (Isa. 63:13).
- He is in us; Jesus is in us (1 Cor. 6:19).
- He is grieved (Eph. 4:30).
- Spirit "Himself" bears witness (Rom. 8:16).
- The Spirit loves (Rom. 5:5, 15:30).
- The Spirit fellowships with us (Phil. 2:1).
- The Holy Spirit comforts us (Acts 9:31).
- He speaks logically to believers and commissions them (Acts 13:2, 4, 21:11).
- The Spirit speaks (Acts 8:29, 28:25).
- The Spirit has a will (1 Cor. 12:11; Heb. 2:4).
- He helps our infirmities (Rom. 8:26).

Holy Spirit Is God

The Holy Spirit has characteristics of God and is equal to God in the scriptures:

- The Father and the Spirit send Jesus (Isa. 48:16).
- The Spirit of the Lord God (Isa. 61:1).
- He is omnipresent (Ps. 139:7–13).
- Blasphemy can only be against God (Mark 3:29).
- Holy Spirit created in Mary the incarnate god/man (Matt. 1:18).
- To sin against Him is eternal (Matt. 12:31).
- He is omnipotent (Luke 1:35).
- The Lord is the Spirit (2 Cor. 3:17).
- To lie to Holy Spirit is to lie to God, Spirit = God (Acts 5:3–4).
- He is joined with God (Matt. 28:19) and with Jesus (2 Cor. 13:14).

- He is eternal (Heb. 9:14).
- He is omniscient (1 Cor. 2:10–11).
- He is sovereign (1 Cor. 12:6–11).

The Work of Holy Spirit

We cannot see the Holy Spirit, but we can feel His presence and see the work He does.

Jesus said, when describing the Holy Spirit, that we know the wind is there but can't see it. We see the results of the wind's presence.

- Regenerates (John 3:3–5)
- Indwells (Rom. 8:11; John 14)
- Anoints (1 John 2:20, 27)
- Baptizes (Acts 2:17–41)
- Guides (John 16:13)
- Empowers (Mic. 3:8)
- Sanctifies (2 Thess. 2:13; Rom. 15:16)
- Bears witness (Heb. 10:15; Rom. 8:16)
- Gives joy (Rom. 14:17)
- Gives gifts (1 Cor. 12:3–11)
- Bears fruit (Gal. 5:22–23)
- Enlightens (1 Cor. 2:10–13)

God is Spirit—the Greek word for *spirit* is *pneuma*.

Pneuma (from *Strong's Concordance* number 376) means "spirit" in Greek. In Luke 24:39, Jesus stated, "A pneuma does not have flesh and bones, as you observe me having." Thus, Jesus defined *pneuma* as a living being without a body. James 2:26, referring to humans, says, "The body without the pneuma is dead." (James did *not* write that the pneuma was dead.) In the New Testament, *pneuma* usually represents a living, nonphysical being or a nonphysical part of a human.

The Names of the Lord Jesus Christ

Jesus is God in human form (2 Cor. 4:4; Heb. 1:4; John 14:9; John 1:1). He took on a human form and functioned as a human to pay the price for sin.

1. Lord, kurios, emphasizes the authority of God. This is His divine title; it emphasizes His deity.
2. Jesus's name in Hebrew is Joshua, which means "Jehovah saves." This is His human name; it may emphasize His humanity.
3. Christ in Greek means "anointed," and Messiah in Hebrew means "the anointed one." A symbol of Holy Spirit is the anointing oil which flows down and soaks into a person, representing the Holy Spirit infilling a person. Jesus was filled without measure. He restored man's spiritual side, which emphasizes His purpose.
4. It is respectful to refer to Him by His full title: the Lord Jesus Christ.
5. Son of God emphasizes deity (John 5:18, 10:33).
6. Son of Man emphasizes humanity.
7. Son of David—He is King of the Jews on the throne of David forever.
8. The last Adam (1 Cor. 15:45).
9. Advocate (1 John 2:1).
10. Amen (Rev. 3:14).
11. Beginning of the creation of God (Rev. 3:14).
12. Branch (Zech. 3:8, 6:12).

13. Bright and morning star (Rev. 22:16).
14. Cornerstone (1 Pet. 2:6).
15. Day spring (Luke 1:78).
16. Deliverer (Rom. 11:26).
17. Elohim (Isa. 40:3, 9:6, 7; John 20:28; Titus 1:3, 2:13; Rom. 15:6; Eph. 1:3, 5:5, 20; 2 Pet. 1:1; 1 John 5:20; Rom. 9:5).
18. Emmanuel God with us (Matt. 1:23).
19. The faithful and true (Rev. 19).
20. First and last (Rev. 1:8, 17).
21. First begotten from the dead (Rev. 1:5).
22. High priest (Heb. 5:1, 5).
23. Holy one (Luke 4:34; Acts 3:14).
24. Image of God (2 Cor. 4:4).
25. Jehovah (Zech. 12:10; Jer. 23:5–6; Ps. 68:18; Eph 4:8–10; Ps. 102:12; Heb. 1:10; Rev. 1:22; Mal 3:1).
26. Just one (Acts 3:14, 7:52).
27. King of Israel (John 1:49).
28. King of the Jews (Matt. 2:2).
29. King of Kings (Rev. 17:14).
30. Lamb of God (John 1:29; Rev. 5:6).
31. Light true (John 1:8–9).
32. Lion of the tribe of Judah (Rev. 5:5).
33. Lord (John 20:28).
34. Lord of Lords (Rev. 17:14).
35. Lord of Glory (1 Cor. 2:8).
36. Lord our righteousness (Jer. 23:6).
37. Maker and preserver of all things (John 1:3; Col. 1:16).
38. Mediator (1 Tim. 2:5; Heb. 12:24).
39. Messiah (John 1:41).
40. Nazarene (Matt. 2:23).

41. Passover (our) (1 Cor. 5:7).
42. Prince of Life (Acts 3:15).
43. Prince of Peace (Isa. 9:6).
44. Prophet (Deut. 18:18; Luke 24:19).
45. Redeemer (Job 19:25).
46. Root of David (Rev. 5:5, 22:16).
47. Ruler of Israel (Mic. 5:2).
48. Savior (Luke 2:11; Acts 5:31).
49. Shepherd (John 10:11; Heb. 13:20).
50. Shiloh (Gen. 49:10).
51. Son of God (Matt. 3:17; Luke 1:32).
52. Son only begotten (John 1:1, 4, 18).
53. Son of Man (Matt. 8:20; John 1:5, 1).
54. Son of David (Matt. 9:27, 21:9).
55. Star and Scepter (Num. 24:17).
56. Way, truth, and life (John 14:6).
57. Witness faithful (Rev. 1:5).
58. The Word (John 1:1; Rev, 19:13).

I like the names Redeemer and Emmanuel because they tell the story of God becoming human, presenting Himself to mankind and offering eternal life to those who accept Him and His plan. He gives a down payment of His Holy Spirit and promises to return later and pick us up. We are now in "layaway," so to speak! Jesus is in heaven, preparing a place for us.

Theologians called it a theophany when God appeared to mankind in the Old Testament. Exploring the circumstances around the spiritual encounter and knowing God's personality can help us better discern what spiritual activity is occurring. Jesus is usually associated with mankind's salvation; the Holy Spirit is associated with sanctification, and

God the Father with creation. Angels are spirit too. We will discuss them and the works of God in later chapters.

The Nature of God

What is the nature of God? The Trinity or nature of God is difficult to understand. We accept the Trinity, but we don't truly fully understand it. How can a person understand how God is one and yet is three distinct persons and not three distinct gods? We live in a very limited world of only three spatial dimensions and one temporal dimension of time. The concept of the Trinity is not a contradiction but a paradox in our three-dimensional realm. Even the laws of grammar are broken when discussing the Trinity. In the original language, God says They *is* when referring to Himself. We see the scriptures speaking in a natural way of the three persons and yet they are all described coequally God. Some groups try to fit God into the realm of our logic. God is very clear on this, and it should be evident that none of us fully understand God (Isa. 55:6–9).

> *For this cause I bow my knees unto the Father of our Lord Jesus Christ, Of whom the whole family in heaven and earth is named, That he would grant you, according to the riches of his glory, to be strengthened with might by his Spirit in the inner man; That Christ may dwell in your hearts by faith; that ye, being rooted and grounded in love, May be able to comprehend with all saints what is the breadth, and length, and depth, and height; And to know the love of*

Christ, which passes knowledge, that ye might be filled with all the fullness of God. (Eph. 3:14–19 KJV)

And he answered, Fear not: for they that be with us are more than they that be with them. And Elisha prayed, and said, LORD, I pray thee, open his eyes, that he may see. And the LORD opened the eyes of the young man; and he saw: and, behold, the mountain was full of horses and chariots of fire round about Elisha. (2 Kings 6:16–17 KJV)

My favorite way to explain the Trinity is to look at mankind. God made mankind in His image, a trinity. We have a physical body, a spirit, and a soul but are one person, not three (Thess. 5:23). We cannot function unless we have all three parts.

The Greek describes the Trinity relationship as "One Ousia (i.e., being), three hypostasis (persons)." Our teaching is that God is one being, existing eternally in three hypostases: Father, Son, and the Holy Spirit. The Nicene Creed of AD 381 made this clear. *Hypostasis* is that without which something cannot be. Without each person of the Trinity, God cannot be the God described by the Word. Prior to this time, a word for *trinity* did not occur. It was not until the issue of "What God do we worship?" that the term came to be.

The Trinity is a concept. The word does not appear in the Bible. Within the unity of the one God there are three persons, the Father, the Son, and the Holy Spirit, and these three share the same nature and attributes. In effect, the three "persons" are the "one God."

The Trinity is not three separate and distinct gods (individuals), which would be tritheism. God is *not* three separate consciousnesses, three separate minds, three separate wills, or three separate forms or bodies.

The Trinity is "one" God composed of three distinct but not separate persons. The problem is with the word *person*. The meaning used by the apostolic fathers was not synonymous with *individual* as it is used today. It is better translated from the Greek *hypostasis*, "mode of being," or *personna*, "manner of subsistence."

The Bible states that God is *one* God. However, it never says that God is *one* person. This is a very important distinction. If God wanted us to think that the Father, the Son, and the Holy Spirit were one person, He would have made it clear and not used the distinctive references to them being distinct from one another in form or manifestation. We see Jesus being baptized, the Holy Spirit coming down from heaven as a dove, and God the Father speaking from heaven, "This is My beloved Son, in whom I am well pleased."

The same is true of the Trinity. In our flesh, limited to a few dimensions of understanding, we cannot understand how the Trinity is valid. Yet we can accept that fact as we study Scripture.

Looking at mankind, who was made in the image of God, we see that we resemble a trinity too! We have a body, a soul, and a spirit but are just one person.

We also know that our abilities are a mere image of God's and we cannot perceive the world from the way God does or understand God as He is. For example, God is "all knowing" and we are not, but we do know some things in part (1 Cor. 13:12). In other words, we reflect His nature but do not fully possess it.

The Westminster Catechism Definition of God

God is a Spirit, in and of himself infinite in being, glory, blessedness, and perfection; all-sufficient, eternal, unchangeable, incomprehensible, everywhere present, almighty, knowing all things, most wise, most holy, most just, most merciful and gracious, long-suffering, and abundant in goodness and truth (Westminster Catechism).

One of the most important things a person should do in life is learn the characteristics and attributes of our Creator. Gaining a true perspective of God will bring us into a closer relationship with Him and reduce fears, worries, and other wasted energy. What a person thinks about God shapes their whole relationship with Him and the rest of their life. What a person thinks God feels toward them determines how close they will grow toward Him. Who we are and what we become cannot be separated from our understanding of God. God has great delight in us, and it is not based on our performance or the work we do! It is not His desire that anyone perishes but that as many as choose His plan for salvation may obtain life eternal and glory in heaven.

How can you know God if you don't first learn about Him and His ways, spend time with Him, and develop a relationship? To know Him is to love Him. Once you know and love Him, you learn to trust Him. Once you trust Him, you will be able to surrender and obey Him. He speaks to us in many ways—i.e., the Bible, circumstances, other believers, visions, dreams (Acts 2:17), and the church, to mention a few.

When He draws us, we seek Him. Jesus said, "No one can come to Me unless the Father draws them" (John 6:44). Only the Holy Spirit can reveal the truth in Christ (John 15:26, 16:13; Matt. 16:16). When we seek Him with our whole heart, we find Him (Matt. 7:7; Luke 11:9). When we find Him, He invites us to join Him in His work. We usually have to adjust our lives in order to join Him (Luke 8:15, 11:28; Rev. 3:10). This requires sacrifice for us and those around us. Noah had to build the arc, Abram had to move from Ur, and David had to fight Goliath. Jesus; His mother, Mary; and His friends all suffered. If the price is too high and we cannot adjust our lives to join Him, then He sometimes withdraws for a season. He has no pleasure in us when we draw back (Heb. 10:38). When we finally realize we must totally surrender and trust Him, He returns and invites us to join Him again. We get to know God through this process of obedience. We carry His Word within us, but He leads us into meaningful work and deserves all the credit (John 15:5).

The Examples of God Found in Nature

The number 1 has attributes of God.

Mathematics is a pure, precise, and perfect language, and likewise, so is God. God often uses numbers in the Bible to demonstrate truth. In Genesis 1:1, the first thing mentioned is God. The first number is 1 and has many characteristics of God. The Trinity nature of God is not triplex, $1 + 1 + 1 = 3$, but triune, $1 \times 1 \times 1 = 1$. The number 1 is the only number that reflects the Trinity characteristic of God. Also, God is not a finite man but infinite in nature, and infinity divided by three is still infinity.

God is everywhere present, and the number 1 can be said to be everywhere too. Anything multiplied or divided by 1 stays the same and can be said to be part of everything. It is not only true with all numbers, but creation too. If you say "a tree," it is assumed to be one tree. Or $1 \times \text{tree} = \text{tree}$.

Light has attributes of God.

God calls Himself light, and in nature we know that light behaves with characteristics of both waves and particles at the same time. This would be a contradiction if it were not for measurable facts. So it is a paradox. We cannot understand fully how this is, yet we see it behaving in this way. Therefore, since we cannot understand how light behaves this way, we can only accept that it in fact does. We will go into more detail about light in chapter 4. A time may come when science fully understands why light behaves as it does. In like manner, a day will come when we will fully understand our God when we are in His presence.

> For the invisible things of him from the creation of the world are clearly seen, being understood by the things that are made, even his eternal power and Godhead; so that they are without excuse. (Rom. 1:20 KJV)

Water has attributes of God.

In nature we see evidence of the Trinity with water. In nature it is a well-known fact of chemistry that plain water, when placed in a vacuum under 230 millimeters of gas pressure and at a temperature of zero degrees centigrade, solidifies into ice at the bottom of the container, remains liquid in the center, and vaporizes at the top. At a given instant, the same water is solid, liquid, and gas, yet all three are forms or manifestations of the same basic substance or nature. H_2O, or water, has three forms, ice, liquid, and gas, depending on the temperature. Water vapor, or gas, is invisible, found everywhere, and cannot be felt similar to God the Father, who is invisible and found everywhere. The Holy Spirit is said to flow like water but is also invisible and can be felt. Jesus was

God with us in a visible, tangible, solid form that can be seen and felt; He is Emanuel, which means God with us.

God has attributes of Magnetism

In Nature we know molecules of certain ferrous metals can be aligned and become magnetized to attract other ferrous metals and in like manner preaching the gospel can attract and save souls.

The alignment of these molecules is accomplished by an invisible field passing around the metal, and in like manner, the invisible Holy Spirit is able to convert a soul and polarize it in Christ. They become like a new creature. If a magnet is rubbed on a nonferrous surface, nothing happens, but if rubbed on a ferrous surface, it, too, becomes a magnet. Just like preaching the gospel can polarize some people toward Christ and some not. The three groups of people are (1) those that are polarized to Christ, (2) those that are not, and (3) those that are polarized toward evil.

Just as wood or nonferrous metal can never be magnetized, so some people will never receive the truth, change their hearts, and trust in Jesus.

1. Just as only ferrous materials containing iron or certain alloys can be magnetized, so also only humble, repentant people chosen by God can be born again.
2. Just as electricity flowing around a bar of iron can polarize each molecule north to south, so also can the Word of God and the Holy Spirit transform a person to love good and hate sin.
3. Just as a magnet has an invisible field around it, the church aligned on Jesus has invisible Holy Spirit power.

4. Just as electricity polarizes the iron, the Holy Spirit polarizes the church.

5. Just as joining two polarized molecules together forms a magnet with a field, so too, when two Christians join together, Jesus is in the midst of them.

6. Just as when a magnet joined to a ferrous nonmagnet the two transforms into one larger magnet with a field around both, so also can Christians pass salvation onto other non-Christians. The wife is sanctified by the husband.

7. As a battery's voltage determines how strong the magnet, so does the pastors anointing determine how strong the church characteristics is.

8. Just as removing the voltage from a magnet causes the field to become weaker, removing the pastor from a church will cause less power in the church (residual magnetism).

9. Just as a strong magnet has every molecule aligned to the north, a strong church has every member aligned on Jesus. No hidden agendas.

10. Just as striking an iron bar when it points north polarizes it into a magnet, so too can a person be repolarized by trauma.

11. Just as stroking an iron bar with a magnet will magnetize it, so can keeping company with other Christians pass on the anointing to others.

God has attributes of snowflakes.

Like God, snowflakes are infinite in nature, are all different, and are perfect in symmetrical geometric design. He has made us in His image like snowflakes.

Symbols of the Trinity

Two-dimensional symbols used to represent the Trinity are a ring to represent the never-ending eternal nature of God, a triangle that depicts the Father, Son, and Holy Spirit, the Trinity, and a combination of these two symbols.

The three-dimensional symbol of the Trinity is often depicted as a cube. The presence of God in the temple was in the holy of holies, which was a cubical room at the far west end of the temple.

The Attributes of God

God has a personality, likes, and dislikes, just as we do. See below for a list of His attributes.

The Goodness of God

The goodness of God is His nature, and He delights to be kind, benevolent, cordial, and full of goodwill for mankind. He is tenderhearted and of quick sympathy. His unfailing attitude toward moral beings is open, frank, and friendly. He takes great pleasure in our well-being and is quick to bestow generous blessings on mankind. Jesus came that we might have life more abundantly. God's plan is to redeem us and save us from this broken world (Exod. 33:19; Rom. 8:32, 5:8; James 1:17–18; Ps. 84:11).

The Sovereignty of God

God is sovereign. He is the supreme ruler who has the ultimate power over all. Here are some of the scriptures that describe His sovereignty.

He existed before creation.

> *Before the mountains were brought forth, or ever thou hadst formed the earth and the world, even from everlasting to everlasting, thou art God. (Ps. 90:2 KJV)*

> *For by him were all things created, that are in heaven, and that are in earth, visible and invisible, whether they be thrones, or dominions, or principalities, or powers: all things were created by him, and for him. (Col. 1:1)*

> *Who only hath immortality, dwelling in the light which no man can approach unto; whom no man hath seen, nor can see: to whom be honour and power everlasting. Amen. (1 Tim. 6:16 KJV)*

> *I am Alpha and Omega, the beginning and the ending, saith the Lord, which is, and which was, and which is to come, the Almighty. (Rev. 1:8 KJV)*

He created all things.

> *In the beginning God created the heaven and the earth. (Gen. 1:1 KJV)*

> *All things were made by him; and without him was not anything made that was made. (John 1:3 KJV)*

He upholds all things, sustains all things, and holds things together.

> *For by him were all things created, that are in heaven, and that are in earth, visible and invisible, whether they be thrones, or dominions, or principalities, or powers: all things were created by him, and for him. (Col. 1:16 KJV)*

> *Who being the brightness of his glory, and the express image of his person, and upholding all things by the word of his power, when he had by himself purged our sins, sat down on the right hand of the Majesty on high. (Heb. 1:3 KJV)*

He is above all things.

> *I am the LORD, and there is none else, there is no God beside me: I girded thee, though thou hast not known me: That they may know from the rising of the sun, and from the west, that there is none beside me. I am*

the LORD, and there is none else. I form the light, and create darkness: I make peace, and create evil: I the LORD do all these things. Drop down, ye heavens, from above, and let the skies pour down righteousness: let the earth open, and let them bring forth salvation, and let righteousness spring up together; I the LORD have created it. (Isa. 45:5 KJV)

One God and Father of all, who is above all, and through all, and in you all. (Eph. 4:6 KJV)

He knows all things.

O LORD, thou hast searched me, and known me. Thou knowest my downsitting and mine uprising, thou understandest my thought afar off. Thou compassest my path and my lying down, and art acquainted with all my ways. For there is not a word in my tongue, but, lo, O LORD, thou knowest it altogether. Thou hast beset me behind and before, and laid thine hand upon me. Such knowledge is too wonderful for me; it is high, I cannot attain unto it. Whither shall I go from thy spirit? or whither shall I flee from thy presence? (Ps. 139:1 KJV)

Declaring the end from the beginning, and from ancient times the things that are not yet done, saying, My counsel shall stand, and I will do all my pleasure. (Isa. 46:10 KJV)

He can do all things.

> *Behold, I am the LORD, the God of all flesh: is there anything too hard for me? (Jer. 32:27 KJV)*

> *For with God nothing shall be impossible. (Luke 1:37 KJV)*

He accomplishes all things.

> *The LORD of hosts hath sworn, saying, Surely as I have thought, so shall it come to pass; and as I have purposed, so shall it stand. (Isa. 14:24 KJV)*

> *Declaring the end from the beginning, and from ancient times the things that are not yet done, saying, My counsel shall stand, and I will do all my pleasure. (Isa. 46:10 KJV)*

> *In whom also we have obtained an inheritance, being predestinated according to the purpose of him who worketh all things after the counsel of his own will. (Eph. 1:11 KJV)*

He rules over all things.

> *Thine, O LORD, is the greatness, and the power, and the glory, and the victory, and the majesty: for all that is in the heaven and in the earth is thine; thine is the kingdom, O LORD, and thou art exalted as head above*

all. Both riches and honour come of thee, and thou reignest over all; and in thine hand is power and might; and in thine hand it is to make great, and to give strength unto all. (1 Chron. 29:11–12 KJV)

And at the end of the days I Nebuchadnezzar lifted up mine eyes unto heaven, and mine understanding returned unto me, and I blessed the most High, and I praised and honoured him that liveth forever, whose dominion is an everlasting dominion, and his kingdom is from generation to generation: And all the inhabitants of the earth are reputed as nothing: and he doeth according to his will in the army of heaven, and among the inhabitants of the earth: and none can stay his hand, or say unto him, What doest thou? (Dan. 4:34 KJV)

He is in control of all things, including kings, countries, human events, good angels, Satan, fallen angels, and human decisions.

The king's heart is in the hand of the LORD, as the rivers of water: he turneth it whithersoever he will. (Prov. 21:1 KJV)

For he spake, and it was done; he commanded, and it stood fast. The LORD bringeth the counsel of the heathen to nought: he maketh the devices of the people of none effect. (Ps. 33:9–10 KJV)

Now there was a day when the sons of God came to present themselves before the LORD, and Satan came also among them. And the LORD said unto Satan, Whence comest thou? Then Satan answered the LORD, and said, "From going to and fro in the earth, and from walking up and down in it." ...And the LORD said unto Satan, "Behold, all that he hath is in thy power; only upon himself put not forth thine hand." (Job: 1:6–7, 12 KJV)

And we know that all things work together for good to them that love God, to them who are the called according to his purpose. For whom he did foreknow, he also did predestinate to be conformed to the image of his Son, that he might be the firstborn among many brethren. Moreover, whom he did predestinate, them he also called: and whom he called, them he also justified: and whom he justified, them he also glorified. (Rom. 8:28–30 KJV)

The Holiness of God

There are many facets of holiness. As we start peeling through the layers of understanding, we first started with the definition of *holiness*, then waded through the scriptures to discover that God commands us to be holy as He is holy. God reveals holiness through the law, His Word, His wrath, and His judgment. Thank God for His balancing mercy and love.

1. Holiness is to be set apart from the common, separate from, different, distinct, and unique.

2. Holiness is to be sinless, pure, sacred, untainted; we find there is none like God in the universe.

3. God asks us to be holy and not conform to this world (1 Pet. 1:14; 2 Cor. 6:14–18).

4. God's holiness is satisfied through the work of Jesus Christ, who paid the price for all sin so that mankind is justified in the sight of God. Through one man sin came into the world, and through one man (Jesus) sin is excused.

5. We are progressively becoming more holy year by year as we learn to apply Jesus's message.

6. The Holy Spirit leads us gently through the process of holiness (1 Tim. 4:15, called sanctification).

7. The final step of becoming holy is called glorification, when we get our new bodies in heaven.

8. The process often consists of commitment, obedience, and a change in thinking and attitude.

9. Two areas that most people have trouble with are money and sexual sin.

It is not wise to look back at past sins in our lives, because we are not defined by past mistakes, but we look forward to the goal of holiness, sharing the improvements and progress as we all mature.

There needs to be a balance between earthly concerns and heavenly concerns. Putting God first, trusting Him in all things, is pleasing to Him. God asks us to be holy, and the only way we can do this is through accepting the work of Jesus and receiving the Holy Spirit.

The Wisdom of God

God is all knowing and is in the past, present, and future at the same time. God's wisdom, therefore, is infinite also. He alone can see the results of each decision made by everyone on earth. Because of his nature, God will bring about the best possible result, by the best possible means, for the most possible people, for the longest possible time. There may be many things in our lives that we would like to change. But what if we understood and accepted these things as necessary for some unknown reason to us knowing that God is in charge? Probably to fulfill God's plan for our future good or someone else's good. We all can look back in our lives and see the good that came out of what we thought at that time was a bad situation. Our wisdom is based on our knowledge and experience. God's wisdom sees everything in focus, past, present, and future, each in proper relationship to all, and thus, from His perspective, is able to work toward His predestined goals of present good and everlasting well-being for each of us.

So what do we do? We need to train ourselves to trust in God and seek His wisdom.

1. We find His wisdom in nature. The ant works, the beaver builds, the plants grow, and the weather patterns seem chaotic but water the earth. There is beauty and synergism.
2. We find the wisdom of God in His inspired Written Word. God shows us His plans for the nations, His

plans for mankind's salvation, and God even shows us the future through prophecy. These plans will be examined in chapters 4 and 6.

3. We find His wisdom in Jesus Christ. Jesus became our wisdom from God (1 Cor. 1:30). Jesus teaches us how to live wisely through His parables and teaching.

Wise living begins with reverence for God, spending time with Him, asking for His wisdom (James 1:5).

The Justice of God

God is fair, impartial, lawful, and righteous. He has integrity and is just. So why do bad things happen to good people and good things seem to happen to bad people?

1. We live in a broken world containing evil now, but God provides a way back to eternal life in heaven if we choose (2 Cor. 5:10). This is justice at work.

2. God is able to change what seems to be bad into something good.

3. Our perception of what is good and what is bad is distorted because we don't know the final results in the future.

4. Some things that are perceived bad may give us opportunity to do good.

5. There is an unwritten law of cause and effect. What goes around comes around.

6. The justice of God requires satisfaction and demands punishment. This resulted in Jesus dying

on the cross to pay for the sin of mankind. God's goodness rescued us, and His justice was satisfied.

7. God will judge all the people of the world and give out what we deserve (1 Cor. 3:10).

8. Trust God and rest in His justice, forgiving those around you.

The Love of God

God's extreme love is huge! Once you experience God's love, it changes you forever. Even the hardest heart melts under the wonderful experience. The best description is the Greek word *agape*. God's love is giving, sacrificial, unconditional, and boundless. It is not based on performance! God's love, like rain, falls on the righteous and the wicked. His love has the elements of being tough and yet complete, which means it includes selective correction to keep us on track. No English word can describe God's love.

> *That Christ may dwell in your hearts by faith; that ye, being rooted and grounded in love, May be able to comprehend with all saints what is the breadth, and length, and depth, and height; And to know the love of Christ, which passeth knowledge, that ye might be filled with all the fullness of God. (Eph. 3:17–19 KJV)*

> *For whom the Lord loveth he chasteneth, and scourgeth every son whom he receiveth. (Heb. 12:6 KJV)*

God's love works together with His goodness, His mercy, His long-suffering, and His grace to maximize our highest good. He takes pleasure in each of us for who we are, separate from our performance (Rom. 5:8). In Luke 15, Jesus tells three stories about how God acts and feels when a lost sheep is found, a lost coin is found, and a lost son returns. Jesus reflected God's love to everyone around Him. We are sealed with the Holy Spirit, and through the Holy Spirit, we can reflect God's love to others (1 John 3:16–18). God is love.

> I reap love when I sow it.
> I see love when I show it.
> I feel love when I give it.
> I am love when I live it.
> Loving others sets me free.
> Loving you brings love to me.
>
> —source unknown

The Liberty of God

Sin has kept mankind in bondage, and where there is sin, there are consequences. But the work of Jesus has made available freedom from sin and peace. God gives all believers the gift of the Holy Spirit and puts His laws into our hearts. And where the Sprit is, there is liberty.

> *Restore to me the joy of Your salvation, And uphold me by your generous Spirit. (Ps. 51:12 KJV)*

Now the Lord is that Spirit: and where the Spirit of the Lord is, there is liberty. (2 Cor. 3:17 KJV)

While observing children playing at a local spring, I saw some who were not having fun. They were fearful that they were going to get hurt or break the many rules posted around the pool area. Their parents were constantly yelling at them to stop running, come get sunblock or insect repellant now, watch where they were going, not jump into shallow water, etc. The lifeguards often blew their whistles at the least hint of any danger. Drama and trauma everywhere! These kids were too afraid to have fun.

Then in contrast, I saw some children who were enjoying the springs. They were quick to make friends. They were laughing and playing together, catching minnows or looking for sharks' teeth in the spring's gravelly bottom. They seemed to know all the rules without reading the many signs or being told. They were going from one adventure to the next in great excitement. As they came back and forth to the parents' blanket for a drink or snack, they got a squirt of sunblock or insect repellant. No harsh words were heard, and there was peace. There was freedom to enjoy God's creation in nature.

I want to go through life having one adventure after another like the peaceful children. As we mature, we learn God's law, we learn to trust Him, and we develop faith that God is in control. God promises to put His law into our hearts and gives us peace. He promises us rest. I believe He works in the background beyond our perception, leading us through life and shielding us from evil.

For the LORD God is a sun and shield; The LORD will give grace and glory; No good thing will He withhold from those who walk uprightly. (Ps. 84:11 KJV)

For You, O LORD, will bless the righteous; With favor You will surround him as with a shield. (Ps. 5:12 KJV)

I will put My law in their minds, and write it on their hearts; and I will be their God, and they shall be My people. (Jer. 31:33 KJV)

The LORD is my rock and my fortress and my deliverer; My God, my strength, in whom I will trust; My shield and the horn of my salvation, my stronghold. (Ps. 18:2 KJV)

As for God, His way is perfect; The word of the LORD is proven; He is a shield to all who trust in Him. (Ps. 18:30 KJV)

God Is Faithful

God's faithfulness offers hope for every person no matter what is going on in their life! Keep yourself from getting angry with God for your circumstances. God is faithful to keep score and is faithful to repay in the long run. He is not surprised when we fail and is always faithfully there to pick us up and set us back on track when we come to Him. His creation even shows His faithfulness. The sun comes up every day, gravity always pulls us to the Earth, and all the other laws of nature continue assuring us of God's faithfulness. God is steadfast in affection and allegiance. He is loyal, dependable, and firm in adhering to promises or observing duty. He shows His faithfulness through the lives of His people by keeping His promises (Gen. 12:1–3; Matt. 16:18). God shows us His faithfulness through the Holy Spirit (John 14:15–18; Gal. 5:22–23).

When we are young, our carnal nature leads us into self-centeredness, trusting in ourselves, and trusting in money. The spiritual realm of the kingdom of God gives from abundance, like the feeding of the five thousand, where twelve baskets of leftovers were gathered afterward. Jesus demonstrated that there is more than enough in God's kingdom. Not so in this world, where there is always lack. When we join God's family, we have access to the kingdom resources (the grace of God) through faith. In other words, money buys things on earth, and faith buys things in heaven. Faith is like spiritual money.

All of God's acts are consistent with all His attributes working together to be the immutable godhead. You can't manipulate God. God's character does not depend on his creation. It rains on the just and the unjust as well, showing His faithfulness. You may get a surprise when trusting in worldly things, but God is different. He will not let you down. He is as solid as a rock. All His promises have come to pass or will come to pass. He is faithful to complete what He says. God shows his faithfulness in His Word (Isa. 55:10–11; Titus 1:2; Heb. 6:18). When we take in the Word of God, He is faithful to make it grow into sanctification (John 17:17).

God demonstrates faithfulness when we are weak, when we are tempted, when we sin, and when we fail (2 Cor. 12:9–10; 1 Cor. 10:13; 1 John 1:9; and 2 Tim. 2:11–13). God will not give up on us no matter what we have thought, said, or done. He may draw back for a season if we reject His council, but He always comes back.

John 4 shows the many attributes of God.

Jesus is a picture of the Father (John 14). Jesus displayed the attributes of God in the New Testament in several places. See the story of the woman at the well and note how Jesus treated her, displaying the many attributes of God (John 4). The concern for her welfare showed goodness; He knew all her sins and weaknesses, showing His sovereignty. She sensed His holiness. He displayed wisdom in addressing her questions and faithfully led her to salvation. Jesus was merciful, just, honest, and fair in addressing her problems. She sensed His love, patience, and truthfulness. The truth set her free. Her report led to the salvation of her townspeople.

Divine Completeness and Perfection of God

God is all knowing, everywhere present, and all powerful. God is made up of three persons, the Father, Son, and Holy Spirit. God is love (1 John 4:8), light (1 John 1:5), and Spirit (1 John 4:24).

God Is Love

The first time I felt God's love may have been when I experienced my first puppy love. For me it was about third grade when I felt the overwhelming desire to be close to a girl, walking her to school and writing notes to her during class. What a wonderful feeling! I remember how giddy I felt and how I wanted to show off in front of her. Now, I get the same feelings when I help someone in need. It is as if we feel God's love for the needy or His satisfaction in what we are doing.

51

Another example of God's love is found in nature. Is it not wonderful how God feeds and clothes all the animals, fish, insects, and plants in the world? It is amazing to see each species surviving over great lengths of time. What a miracle of synergism and habitat! And who can refute the special love a dog has for his master? A dog's love has been shown to have a healing effect on people. A dog will often give his life for his master.

God Is Light

Since God calls Himself light, let's examine the attributes of light. There are three different kinds of light discussed in the Bible. We are all familiar with the light from the sun and stars, which are sources of light, and the moon, which reflects light; but there is spiritual light or enlightenment from God and is often equated to his glory or knowledge.

> *This then is the message which we have heard of him, and declare unto you, that God is light, and in him is no darkness at all. (1 John 1:5 KJV)*

> *And the city had no need of the sun, neither of the moon, to shine in it: for the glory of God did lighten it, and the Lamb is the light thereof. (Rev. 21:23 KJV)*

> *For God, who commanded the light to shine out of darkness, hath shined in our hearts, to give the light of the knowledge of the*

*glory of God in the face of Jesus Christ. (2
Cor. 4:6 KJV)*

*For the invisible things of him from the cre-
ation of the world are clearly seen, being
understood by the things that are made, even
his eternal power and Godhead; so that they
are without excuse. (Rom. 1:20 KJV)*

Webster defines *light* as (1) electromagnetic waves that
travel 186,270 miles per second, (2) radiant energy that acts
on the retina of the eye, and (3) knowledge, information,
illumination of the mind.

Scientists don't really know what light is. It travels
through space and is invisible until it is reflected off some
substance. It acts both like a particle and a wave. It vibrates at
different frequencies to generate different colors. May I suggest that God is an invisible Spirit in this earthly realm?
Unless He is reflected off someone! When we demonstrate
godly behavior, like loving one another, good moral behavior, or show our love toward God in worship, we reflect His
love. Light can be absorbed, and the blessings of God can be
absorbed, changing us into the image of Jesus.

Scientists characterize light by measuring the packets of
energy, called photons, and quantify light by measuring its
heat in units of calories. They have learned to focus and
amplify light using lenses and lasers. Laser light can be used
to cut off unwanted tissue, or expanded to illuminate large
areas using floodlights. Likewise, the church knows God's
Word is sharper than a two-edged sword and cuts spiritually,
can be spread over a large area by enlightening the masses
with the gospel, and can be focused down to an individual

when praying for the sick. God cannot be manipulated but is willing to partner with the church if it operates out of love.

When mixing source light like beams of photons in a television, the most common set of primary colors is red (R), green (G), and blue (B). When red, green, and blue light are mixed or added together with the same intensity, white (W) light is obtained. Yellow photons mixed with blue photons make the color red. The addition of these three primary colors of light with varying degrees of intensity will result in the countless other colors that we see and are familiar with. TV screens use this source light to get different colors by mixing different colors (wavelengths of light) together.

Reflected light that we usually see in the world obeys different rules. It is like mixing paint or printer ink; the three secondary colors, magenta, cyan, and yellow, mixed together makes black, not white. Yellow mixed with blue makes green. It is interesting that we don't see light unless it bounces off an object. Just like we don't see holiness, love, justice, or any other attribute of God unless it is displayed through someone.

Jesus said He was the light of the world. It became dark when Jesus was on the cross between twelve noon and 3:00 p.m. The absence of light is darkness. History shows that the Dark Ages came about when the gospel was suppressed. But when the Gutenberg Press was invented, Bibles were produced for everyone and the truth of God was being preached by Luther, Calvin, and John Wesley to the world, moving us into Reformation. Great scientific discoveries were made, great musical symphonies were created, Industrial Revolution started to form, and many breakthroughs in medicine were made.

When Jesus asked what people said about Him and Peter replied that he thought Jesus was the Son of God, Jesus replied that God (Holy Spirit) had revealed this to Him.

> *Then spake Jesus again unto them, saying, I am the light of the world: he that followeth me shall not walk in darkness, but shall have the light of life. (John 8:12 KJV)*

> *Then Jesus said unto them, Yet a little while is the light with you. Walk while ye have the light, lest darkness come upon you: for he that walketh in darkness knoweth not whither he goeth. While ye have light, believe in the light, that ye may be the children of light. (John 12:35–36 KJV)*

God Is Spirit

The Holy Spirit of God is often depicted flowing like water or blowing like the wind. The anointing oil is a symbol of the Holy Spirit and was used to anoint prophets, kings, and priests in the Old Testament of the Bible. It flowed over the head and dripped off the beard. Oil soaks into the skin, cleansing and nourishing the body. It becomes part of the person. I believe baptism involves water for the same reasons, and in Communion the bread feeds the physical body while the wine feeds the spiritual part of mankind.

Conclusion

In this chapter we have examined who God is according to the Bible by looking at the meanings of God's names, His nature, and His attributes. You can tell much about the artist by looking at his work, so we have looked into nature to find similarities that may reveal more mysteries about God. Last, we examined the attributes of what God calls Himself, love, light, and Spirit.

In the next chapter, we will look further into God's work of creation and glean more truth about reality. We will examine the earth, mankind, heaven, and angels. We will look at what the Bible says about the different realms of reality. We will find information about why Jesus told Nicodemus that you have to be born again to see and enter the kingdom of God. And why God said, "Let there be light," on the first day and made the sun, moon, and stars on the fourth day.

> *For the invisible things of him from the creation of the world are clearly seen, being understood by the things that are made, even his eternal power and Godhead; so that they are without excuse. (Rom. 1:20 KJV)*

CHAPTER 2

Creation

The Creation Story

I n the beginning God created the heavens and the earth (Gen. 1:1). Since God dwells in eternity outside of time and is in the past, present, and future at the same time, it is difficult for mankind to put a timeline on God's work. From mankind's perspective time seems to be ongoing, constantly unfolding. From God's perspective, time is like a tape measure. God sees the past and future all at once. God says He is in eternity, outside of time as we know it. He is the Alpha and Omega, the beginning and the end. Two places in the Bible say that to God one day is as one thousand years (Ps. 90:4; 2 Pet. 3:8). God made the Earth in six days and rested the seventh day, and this seven-thousand-year pattern seems to be His calendar for planet Earth activity.

We are told that God is perfect and creates only perfect things. The universe was a perfect and beautiful place after He formed it. He filled heaven with angels and the earth with a complex array of minerals, plants, insects, animals, and people. The earth definitely shows a complex design, and where there is a design, there is a designer. Some scholars have a long creation perspective and believe there may have been a large time gap between Genesis 1:1 and Genesis 1:2. Something may have happened to God's perfect creation in this time gap, for it was described as dark, void, without form, and covered by water. God has demonstrated complete control over time. He says He redeems time, shortens time, and extends time.

> *In the beginning God created the heaven and the earth. 1:2 And the earth was without form, and void; and darkness was upon the face of the deep. And the Spirit of God moved upon the face of the waters. (Gen. 1:1 KJV)*

I believe that the Bible's account of creation is true and that the Earth is young based on evidence of human artifacts found in almost all rock stratum that are supposed to be millions of years apart. Likewise, tree trunks have been found growing through different stratum of rock that are supposed to be millions of years apart. Evidence of the flood depositing silt in layers all over the earth, creating each stratum, looks more likely. The dust on the moon was found to be only a couple of inches deep, supporting a young creation. The moon's orbit is expanding at a constant rate and also supports a young creation. River delta silt throughout the world rivers shows deposits for about four thousand years. Even footprints of dinosaur and mankind are found together in the same place and time in Texas. The Grand Canyon and the Columbia River gorge may have been carved out quickly when vast lakes were funneled through them after the Ice Age. What is true is that God is real and can do anything since He is all-powerful and all-knowing and doesn't lie. He is able to keep His Word (the Bible) from error.

The Gospel Story Told in the Star Constellations

Long before men perverted the message of the constellations and established ancient idolatry, God named the stars and set them in the heavens for signs:

> *And God said, Let there be lights in the firmament of the heaven to divide the day from the night; and let them be for signs, and for seasons, and for days, and years (Gen. 1:14 KJV).*

The book of Job predates the writing of Genesis. Though it is part of the Bible, it was written about a man who lived before Moses. Job had no written Bible. The Bible this ancient pilgrim read consisted of a series of constellations that appeared in the night skies high above the earth.

There are references to these constellations in the book of Job, along with an explanation of why they appear as they do in the heavens. Job 26 tells us that the "crooked serpent" is one of God's leading characters in this drama of the ages and that these constellations—these "pillars of heaven"—make up the "parts" of God's "ways":

> *The pillars of heaven tremble and are astonished at his reproof...*

> *By his spirit he hath garnished the heavens; his hand hath formed the crooked serpent.*
>
> *Lo, these are parts of his ways. (Job 26:11, 13–14 KJV)*

The Zodiac is the distorted Mazzaroth of Job 38:32 (See Ps. 19, 147; Isa. 13:10, 40:26; Acts 28:1).

- Virgo—the virgin, the promised seed of the woman
- Libra—the scales, the Redeemer's atoning work
- Scorpio—the scorpion, the Redeemer's conflict
- Sagittarius—the archer, the Redeemer's triumph, conquering the devil
- Capricorn—the goat, sacrifice slain for us; our blessings procured
- Aquarius—living water, blessings ensured (Holy Spirit)
- Pisces—the fish, the redeemed blessed, though still bound
- Aries—the lamb, blessings consummated and enjoyed
- Taurus—the bull, the Messiah coming to judge and rule
- Gemini—the twins, the twofold nature of the king (man and God)
- Cancer—the sheepfold, the redeemed held fast (Big Dipper)
- Leo—the lion of the tribe of Judah, Christ's second coming as King

The Sphinx faces east and shows where
the gospel story starts and ends (between
Leo and Virgo the virgin).
(by J. R. Church, July 17, 2011)

Lucifer

What may have happened in this gap of time between
Genesis 1:1 and Genesis 1:2 is not well documented but is
only described briefly in the Bible. Lucifer, described as a
covering cherub created perfect by God, was called the "god
of this world" according to 2 Corinthians 4:4. He was found
in the garden of Eden with Adam and Eve just after 4004 BC
according to Jewish and Roman historians, so he was probably created before mankind. It is very interesting that Lucifer
is described as a very powerful angel in Ezekiel 28 and a
dragon and serpent in Revelation 12:9. It is an archeological
fact that there were dinosaurs (large serpents) living on earth.
Could it be that Lucifer was connected to this age of dinosaurs before the garden of Eden? There is so much we don't
know about our universe, but I suspect it is a more exciting
place than any sci-fi adventure we could imagine.

*In whom the god of this world hath blinded
the minds of them which believe not, lest
the light of the glorious gospel of Christ,
who is the image of God, should shine unto
them. (2 Cor. 4:4 KJV)*

*Thou hast been in Eden the garden of God;
every precious stone [was] thy covering, the*

sardius, topaz, and the diamond, the beryl, the onyx, and the jasper, the sapphire, the emerald, and the carbuncle, and gold: the workmanship of thy tabrets and of thy pipes was prepared in thee in the day that thou was created. Thou [art] the anointed cherub that covereth; and I have set thee [so]: thou wast upon the holy mountain of God; thou hast walked up and down in the midst of the stones of fire. Thou [wast] perfect in thy ways from the day that thou wast created, till iniquity was found in thee. By the multitude of thy merchandise they have filled the midst of thee with violence, and thou hast sinned: therefore, I will cast thee as profane out of the mountain of God: and I will destroy thee, O covering cherub, from the midst of the stones of fire. Thine heart was lifted up because of thy beauty, thou hast corrupted thy wisdom by reason of thy brightness: I will cast thee to the ground, I will lay thee before kings, that they may behold thee. Thou hast defiled thy sanctuaries by the multitude of thine iniquities, by the iniquity of thy traffick; therefore will I bring forth a fire from the midst of thee, it shall devour thee, and I will bring thee to ashes upon the earth in the sight of all them that behold thee. All they that know thee among the people shall be astonished at thee: thou shalt be a terror, and never [shalt] thou [be] any more. (Ezek. 28:13 KJV)

The anointed cherub (Lucifer) was made perfect but became corrupted by pride. In verse 28:18 above, God sets a trap, a dragon trap. God may have used mankind for bait knowing that Satan would try to destroy God's new addition to creation. Since God does not kill, He allowed Satan to destroy himself through an elaborate plan.

> *How art thou fallen from heaven, O Lucifer, son of the morning! how art thou cut down to the ground, which didst weaken the nations! For thou hast said in thine heart, I will ascend into heaven, I will exalt my throne above the stars of God: I will sit also upon the mount of the congregation, in the sides of the north: I will ascend above the heights of the clouds; I will be like the Most High. Yet thou shalt be brought down to hell, to the sides of the pit. They that see thee shall narrowly look upon thee, and consider thee, saying, Is this the man that made the earth to tremble, that did shake kingdoms; That made the world as a wilderness, and destroyed the cities thereof; that opened not the house of his prisoners? All the kings of the nations, even all of them, lie in glory, everyone in his own house. But thou art cast out of thy grave like an abominable branch, and as the raiment of those that are slain, thrust through with a sword, that go down to the stones of the pit; as a carcass trodden under feet. (Isa. 14:12 KJV)*

Lucifer (described as a red dragon with a tail) tried to kill Christ after He was born. But Mary and Joseph escaped to Egypt with Jesus. One-third of the angels may have followed Lucifer, and some were cast down to the earth. Lucifer is now called a serpent, devil, accuser, and Satan, our adversary.

> And there appeared another wonder in heaven; and behold a great red dragon, having seven heads and ten horns, and seven crowns upon his heads.
>
> And his tail drew the third part of the stars of heaven, and did cast them to the earth: and the dragon stood before the woman which was ready to be delivered, for to devour her child as soon as it was born. And she brought forth a man child, who was to rule all nations with a rod of iron: and her child was caught up unto God, and to his throne. And the woman fled into the wilderness, where she hath a place prepared of God, that they should feed her there a thousand two hundred and threescore days. And there was war in heaven: Michael and his angels fought against the dragon; and the dragon fought and his angels, And prevailed not; neither was their place found any more in heaven.
>
> And the great dragon was cast out, that old serpent, called the Devil, and Satan, which deceiveth the whole world: he was cast out into the earth, and his angels were cast out with him.

> *And I heard a loud voice saying in heaven, Now is come salvation, and strength, and the kingdom of our God, and the power of his Christ: for the accuser of our brethren is cast down, which accused them before our God day and night.*
>
> *And they overcame him by the blood of the Lamb, and by the word of their testimony; and they loved not their lives unto the death. (Rev. 12:3 KJV)*

Other Realms

To understand the creation and the kingdoms of God, one must understand the dimensions of reality and the infinite nature of God.

> *For the invisible things of him from the creation of the world are clearly seen, being understood by the things that are made, even his eternal power and Godhead; so that they are without excuse. (Rom. 1:20)*

Perhaps the earth is a shadow of other dimensions that are part of God's kingdoms. The earth has different habitats—the air where birds fly, the water where fish swim, and the land where animals roam. Above the earth in outer space, we are told that angels exist. And then there is heaven, where God dwells, and hell under the earth. The realms that we see may be a shadow of other dimensions that are invisible to us now.

*Through faith we understand that the
worlds were framed by the word of God, so
that things which are seen were not made of
things which do appear. (Heb. 11:3)*

*While we look not at the things which are
seen, but at the things which are not seen:
for the things which are seen are temporal;
but the things which are not seen are eternal. (2 Cor. 4:18)*

Heaven is always plural in the Bible, hinting of the
many layers of reality above our own.

God is infinite in nature and perhaps not fully perceiv-
able from our three-dimensional realm.

Time is related to speed, distance, and it can be distorted by gravity. Time is not a physical dimension but a
temporal dimension.

There are many spatial dimensions. A point is defined
as having no dimensions, a line is made up of an infinite
number of points and is defined as having one dimension, a
plane is made up of an infinite number of lines and is defined
as having two dimensions, a cube is made up of an infinite
number of planes and is defined as having three dimensions,
and a tesseract is made up of an infinite number of cubes and
is defined as having four dimensions. (See tesseract webpage
at https://www.youtube.com/watch?v=iGO12Z5Lw8s.)

Extrapolating the above dimensional patterns gives us
an idea of what heaven may be like or what true reality may
start to look like. If heaven is a higher dimension, it may
explain why flesh and blood cannot inherit the kingdom of
God (1 Cor. 15:50) or how the stars can roll up like a scroll

(Isa. 34:4). Heaven may be an infinite number of earthlike realms!

When Jesus performed miracles, He often declared that the kingdom of God had come close (Matt. 12:28). Moving from one dimension to the next seems to require motion. Moving a line sweeps out a plane, moving a point sweeps out a line, etc. When Jesus performed miracles, He often required people to move: "Stretch forth your hand" or "Go to the pool of Shalom." Notice, too, that the higher dimension still maintains the characteristics of the lower dimensions. In other words, there are lines in a plane and planes in a cube, so when we are changed in the twinkling of an eye, our heavenly bodies will have all the characteristics of our earthly bodies, but more. Jesus was recognized by the disciples, and they could still touch him after His resurrection.

> *While we look not at the things which are seen, but at the things which are not seen: for the things which are seen are temporal; but the things which are not seen are eternal. (2 Cor. 4:18 KJV)*

> *And when he was demanded of the Pharisees, when the kingdom of God should come, he answered them and said, The kingdom of God cometh not with observation: Neither shall they say, Lo here! or, lo there! for, behold, the kingdom of God is within you. (Luke 17:20–22 KJV)*

Maybe the kingdom of God is here now all around us and Jesus was showing us how to access it through Him. He did say He was the way, truth, and life.

Verily, verily, I say unto you, He that believeth on me, the works that I do shall he do also; and greater works than these shall he do; because I go unto my Father. (John 14:12 KJV)

For by him were all things created, that are in heaven, and that are in earth, visible and invisible, whether they be thrones, or dominions, or principalities, or powers: all things were created by him, and for him: And he is before all things, and by him all things consist. (Col 1:16–17 KJV)

God declared who he was to Moses in Exodus 34:6–7. Notice there was no physical description.

And the Lord passed by before him, and proclaimed, The Lord, The Lord God, merciful and gracious, longsuffering, and abundant in goodness and truth, Keeping mercy for thousands, forgiving iniquity and transgression and sin, and that will by no means clear the guilty; visiting the iniquity of the fathers upon the children, and upon the children's children, unto the third and to the fourth generation. (Exod. 34:6 KJV)

But seek ye first the kingdom of God, and his righteousness; and all these things (previously mentioned) shall be added unto you. (Matt. 6:33 KJV)

Numbers in the Bible

There are different levels at which people can study the Bible. Since God is infinite and perfect, it stands to reason He would have layers of information encoded in His Word. The first level of understanding is accomplished by reading the Word of God and believing its literal meaning. A deeper understanding is often reached by cross-referencing other scriptures on the same topic. And deeper still when counting how often a word or phrase is used.

Both the Hebrew and Greek language had no numbers but used letters for numbers like Latin uses Roman numerals. Many psalms in the Bible are numbered by using letters (see Ps. 119), and the Bible tells us that these numbers exist and may be useful in further understanding God's Word.

Numbers and exact measurements were given by God for building the ark, building the tabernacle, and defining the New Jerusalem according to the heavenly patterns.

> *Who serve unto the example and shadow of heavenly things, as Moses was admonished of God when he was about to make the tabernacle: for, See, saith he, that thou make all things according to the pattern showed to thee in the mount. (Heb. 8:5 KJV)*

God even knows the number of the hair on our heads.

> *But, the very hairs of your head are all numbered. (Matt. 10:30 KJV)*

CREATION

But, even the very hairs of your head are all numbered. Fear not therefore: ye are of more value than many sparrows. (Luke 12:7 KJV)

The Bible is full of numerical symbology. We have seen where in the beginning God created the heavens and the earth, so the first thing mentioned in the Bible is God Himself. The first number is 1 and seems to represent God. The number 1 has several attributes of God. God is a trinity and yet only one god, and the number 1 is the only number that can represent this concept (1 x 1 x 1 = 1 and 1 + 1 + 1 = 3). There are patterns of three all through nature that show the fingerprint of the Trinity. We live in three dimensions, thickness, width, and length; past, present, and future; water, land, and air.

The number 4 usually represents the earth and worldly ideas and concepts. Four corners of the earth (north, south, east, and west) and four seasons (summer, fall, winter, and spring).

The number 5 is usually associated with grace, 6 is the number for mankind, and 7 is used in God's Word representing completeness of spiritual things. The number 8 is Jesus's heavenly number of new beginnings and the resurrection. Jesus rose from the dead on Sunday, the eighth day, and eight were saved in the flood (Noah and his family). The number 9 usually is associated with judgment, 10 represents the law, and 12 has to do with perfect government (twelve apostles) or time (twelve hours in a day or twelve months in a year).

When adding up the numerical values of the Greek letters for "Jesus," the number is 888, and likewise the word *cross* is 777. *Truth* is 64, which is 8 x 8. Revelation 13:17–18 introduces us to 666. This may show that the cross is the bridge between good and evil that we must travel. For a more complete understanding of the number 666, read Isaiah 17:4, 2 Samuel 21:20, 1 John 4:3, and Ezekiel 2:13, about the spirit of the antichrist. Studying the Bible by looking at the numerical value of each letter in a word is called gematria. God is sure smart to combine mathematics and words together to tell the same story.

God's Works Show a Pattern of Three

God made the world, and it was good. The sky, water, and land were made from microscopic particles. All matter was made from atoms that have three parts, protons, neutrons, and electrons. Each of these is made up of a triad of quarks and leptons and together makes up the three types of matter (animal, vegetable, or mineral). Time is made up of past, present, and future; our spatial reality is made up of thickness, width, and length. Paul says there are three heavens, the terrestrial, the celestial, and the third heaven, where God dwells (2 Cor. 12:2). The numeral 3 is the number of completeness.

Man is made in God's image, or shadow, three parts, body, spirit, and soul.

> And the LORD God formed man of the dust
> of the ground [body], and breathed into his
> nostrils the breath of life [spirit]. Man
> became a living [soul]. (Gen. 2:7 KJV)

The soul contains our feelings, personality, and imagination.

And the very God of peace sanctify you
wholly; and [I pray God] your whole spirit
and soul and body be preserved blameless
unto the coming of our Lord Jesus Christ.
(Thess. 5:23 KJV)

According to the Zohar, a commentary of the Torah, the soul is thought to reside in the brain and is made up of three parts, one within the other, and the brain resides in the body:

1. Spirit, translated from the Hebrew word *ruah*.
2. Breath of God, translated from the Hebrew word *neshamah* (Gen. 2:7).
3. Soul, translated from the Hebrew word *nephesh* (Gen. 2:7).
4. Flesh, from the Hebrew word *aphar*, formed from the dust (elements) (Gen. 2:7).

I believe that sin separated mankind from God and the neshamah became broken, eventually causing death. But Jesus, the light of the world, restores the neshamah when a person is born again. Our spirit needs the neshamah to live in harmony with God in heaven.

This book describes some of God's plans for the restoration of mankind by looking at the many beautiful patterns in nature that reflect God's works, grace, and love. I believe the man that God made before sin is much more than just a physical body. There is a spiritual part of man that is invisible and eternal. My question is, Why are most scientists looking at ancient bones from physical bodies and determining if it is human? They can't see man's spiritual side by looking at the physical body parts. We are told in Genesis chapter 6 that angels contaminated mankind's DNA before the flood and after. There were monsters like the Nephilim, Ananochi, and legendary Greek gods. There is a spiritual battle going on around us that cannot be perceived by our physical senses, a different reality that Jesus often called the kingdom of God. Jesus said that man doesn't live by bread alone, showing there is more to mankind than physical. The good news is that God wins in the end and eternal life with God is made available for mankind if we choose to believe God and allow Him to fix our broken spirit.

> *For we wrestle not against flesh and blood, but against principalities, against powers, against the rulers of the darkness of this world, against spiritual wickedness in high places. (Eph. 6:12 KJV)*

> *For by him were all things created, that are in heaven, and that are in earth, visible and invisible, whether they be thrones, or dominions, or principalities, or powers: all things were created by him, and for him. (Col. 1:16 KJV)*

Thrones, dominions, principalities, and powers in the above scripture may be types of angels.

Angels

God created the heavens also and filled them. One can only imagine the wonderful things God made in the heavens. It is described as being a spiritual eternal realm and having angels. The Bible describes angels as eternal, celestial, spiritual living beings made by God who are more powerful than mankind. Nowhere are they described as being made in God's image, and they don't seem to comprehend mankind's salvation but are watching as things unfold. They were created to serve God and look after His creation. They were present in heaven before the earth was formed. Large in number and different from one another, they are organized in ranks like a military command. They are sometimes called sons of God because they were made by God. Jesus is God's only begotten son speaking to the virgin birth. Jesus said we have guardian angels assigned to us and over nations.

> *Take heed that ye despise not one of these little ones; for I say unto you, That in heaven their angels do always behold the face of my Father which is in heaven. (Matt. 18:1–10 KJV)*

Angels are also used to enforce judgment at the end of the age.

> *The Son of man shall send forth his angels, and they shall gather out of his kingdom all things that offend, and them which do iniquity. (Matt. 13:41 KJV)*

The Bible and other ancient books hint of a war in heaven before the garden of Eden and a split occurring to the heavenly host, creating both good and bad angels. About one-third of the angels are called fallen angels. Many seem to have the ability to change shape and appear as human or animals (Job 4:18; Matt. 25:41; Col. 1:16; 2 Pet. 2:4; Jude 6; Rev 12:9).

There are different kinds of angels described in the scriptures who are divided by function and their closeness to God.

Seraphim

> *Seraphim* (Hebrew words ending in "im" are plural.) Seraphim are seen around the throne of God.

> > *In the year that king Uzziah died I saw also the Lord sitting upon a throne, high and lifted up, and his train filled the temple. Above it stood the seraphim: each one had six wings; with twain he covered his face, and with twain he covered his feet, and with twain he did fly. And one cried unto another, and said, Holy, holy, holy, [is] the* Lord *of hosts: the whole earth [is] full of his glory. And the posts of the door moved at the voice of him that cried, and the house was filled with smoke., serve as the caretakers of God's throne and continuously shout praises: "Holy, holy, holy is the Lord of hosts. All the earth is filled with His Glory." (Isa 6:1 KJV)*

The name *seraphim* mean "the burning ones." The seraphim have six wings, two covering their faces, two covering their bodies ("feet"), and two with which they fly.

Two of the seraphim are named Seraphiel and Metatron, according to some ancient books. Seraphiel is said to have the head like an eagle. It is said that such a bright light emanates from them that nothing, not even other angelic beings, can look upon them. It is also said that there are four of them surrounding God's throne, where they burn eternally from the love and zeal for God.

Cherubim

Cherubim guard the entrance to the Garden of Eden and God's presence in the Tabernacle Holy of Holies. Satan was a cherub.

> *Thou hast been in Eden the garden of God; every precious stone [was] thy covering, the sardius, topaz, and the diamond, the beryl, the onyx, and the jasper, the sapphire, the emerald, and the carbuncle, and gold: the workmanship of thy tabrets and of thy pipes was prepared in thee in the day that thou wast created. Thou [art] the anointed cherub that covereth; and I have set thee [so]: thou wast upon the holy mountain of God; thou hast walked up and down in the midst of the stones of fire. Thou [wast] perfect in thy ways from the day that thou wast created, till iniquity was found in thee. By the multitude of thy merchandise they have filled the midst of thee with violence, and thou hast sinned: therefore, I will cast thee as profane out of the mountain of God: and I will destroy thee, O covering cherub, from the midst of the stones of fire. Thine heart was lifted up because of thy beauty, thou hast corrupted thy wisdom by reason of thy brightness: I will cast thee to the ground, I will lay thee before kings, that they may*

behold thee. Thou hast defiled thy sanctuar-
ies by the multitude of thine iniquities, by
the iniquity of thy traffick; therefore, will I
bring forth a fire from the midst of thee, it
shall devour thee, and I will bring thee to
ashes upon the earth in the sight of all them
that behold thee. All they that know thee
among the people shall be astonished at
thee: thou shalt be a terror, and never [shalt]
thou [be] any more. (Ezek. 28:13–19 KJV)

Cherubim are depicted as having four faces: one of each a man, an ox, a lion, and a griffon. They have four conjoined wings covered with eyes, and they have ox's feet. Cherubim guarded the way to the tree of life in the garden of Eden (Gen. 3:24) and the throne of God (Ezek. 28:14–16).

The cherubim are mentioned in Genesis 3:24; Exodus 25:17–22; 2 Chronicles 3:7–14; Ezekiel 10:12–14, 28:14–16; 1 Kings 6:23–28; and Revelation 4:6–8.

Modern English usage has blurred the distinction between cherubim and putti. *Putti* are the winged human baby/toddler-like beings traditionally used in figurative art.

The word of the LORD came expressly unto
Ezekiel the priest, the son of Buzi, in the
land of the Chaldeans by the river Chebar;
and the hand of the LORD was there upon
him. And I looked, and, behold, a whirl-
wind came out of the north, a great cloud,
and a fire infolding itself, and a brightness
[was] about it, and out of the midst thereof
as the colour of amber, out of the midst of
the fire. Also out of the midst thereof [came]

the likeness of four living creatures. And this [was] their appearance; they had the likeness of a man. And every one had four faces, and every one had four wings. And their feet [were] straight feet; and the sole of their feet [was] like the sole of a calf's foot: and they sparkled like the colour of burnished brass. And [they had] the hands of a man under their wings on their four sides; and they four had their faces and their wings. Their wings [were] joined one to another; they turned not when they went; they went every one straight forward. As for the likeness of their faces, they four had the face of a man, and the face of a lion, on the right side: and they four had the face of an ox on the left side; they four also had the face of an eagle. Thus [were] their faces: and their wings [were] stretched upward; two [wings] of every one [were] joined one to another, and two covered their bodies. And they went every one straight forward: whither the spirit was to go, they went; [and] they turned not when they went. As for the likeness of the living creatures, their appearance [was] like burning coals of fire, [and] like the appearance of lamps: it went up and down among the living creatures; and the fire was bright, and out of the fire went forth lightning. And the living creatures ran and returned as the appearance of a flash of lightning. Now as I beheld the living creatures, behold one wheel upon the earth by the living creatures, with his four faces. The appearance of the wheels and their work [was] like unto the colour of a beryl: and they four had one likeness: and their appearance and their work [was] as it were a wheel in the middle of a wheel. When they went, they went upon their four sides: [and] they turned not when they went. As for their rings, they were so high that they were dreadful; and their rings [were] full of eyes[12] round about them four. And when the living creatures went, the wheels went by them: and when the living creatures were lifted up from the earth, the wheels were lifted up. Whithersoever the spirit was to go, they went, thither [was their] spirit to go; and the wheels were lifted up over against them: for the spirit of the living creature [was] in the wheels. When those went, [these] went; and when those stood, [these] stood; and when those were lifted up from the earth, the wheels were lifted up over against them: for the spirit of the living creature [was] in the wheels. And the likeness of the firmament upon the heads of the living creature [was] as the colour of the terrible crystal, stretched forth over their heads above. And under the firmament [were] their wings straight, the one toward the other: everyone had two, which covered on this side, and everyone had two, which covered on that side, their bodies. And when they went, I heard the noise of their wings, like the noise of great waters, as the voice of the Almighty, the voice of speech, as the noise of an host: when they stood, they let down their wings. And there was a voice from the firmament that [was] over their heads, when they stood, [and] had let down their wings. (Ezek. 1:3–25 KJV)

Then I looked, and, behold, in the firmament that was above the head of the cherubim there appeared over them as it were a sapphire stone, as the appearance of the likeness of a throne. And he spake unto the man clothed with linen, and said, Go in between the wheels, [even] under the cherub, and fill thine hand with coals of fire from between the cherubim, and scatter [them] over the city. And he went in in my sight. Now the cherubim stood on the right side of the house, when the man went in; and the cloud filled the inner court. Then the glory of the LORD went up from the cherub, [and stood] over the threshold of the house; and the house was filled with the cloud, and the court was full of the brightness of the LORD's glory. And the sound of the cherubims' wings was heard [even] to the outer court, as the voice of the Almighty God when he speaketh. And it came to pass, [that] when he had commanded the man clothed with linen, saying, Take fire from between the wheels, from between the cherubim; then he went in, and stood beside the wheels. And [one] cherub stretched forth his hand from between the cherubim unto the fire that [was] between the cherubim, and took [thereof], and put [it] into the hands of [him that was] clothed with linen: who took [it], and went out. And there appeared in the cherubim the form of a man's hand under their wings. And when I looked, behold the four wheels by the cherubim, one wheel by one cherub, and another wheel by another cherub: and the appearance of the wheels [was] as the colour of a beryl stone. And [as for] their appearances, they four had one likeness, as if a wheel had been in the midst of a wheel. When they went, they went upon their four sides; they turned not as they went, but to the place whither the head looked they followed it; they turned not as they went. And their whole body, and their backs, and their hands, and their wings, and the wheels, [were] full of eyes round about, [even] the wheels that they four had. As for the wheels, it was cried unto them in my hearing, O wheel. And every one had four faces: the first face [was] the face of a cherub, and the second face [was] the face of a man, and the third the face of a lion, and the fourth the face of an eagle. And the cherubim were lifted up. This [is] the living creature that I saw by the river of Chebar. And when the cherubim went, the wheels went by them: and when the cherubim lifted up their wings to mount up from the earth, the same wheels also turned not from beside them. When they stood, [these] stood; and when they were lifted up, [these] lifted up themselves [also]: for the spirit of the living creature [was] in the… Then the glory of the LORD departed from off the threshold of the house, and stood over the cherubim. And the cherubim lifted up their wings, and mounted up from the earth in my sight: when they went out, the wheels also [were] beside them, and [every one] stood at the door of the east gate of the LORD's house; and the glory of the God of Israel [was] over them above. This [is] the living creature that I saw under the God of Israel by the river of Chebar; and I knew that they [were] the cherubim. (Ezek. 10:1–20 KJV)

Eyes—in verse 12 above, the cherubim had many eyes in their wheels, implying they were able to see more of their surroundings or even other dimensions of reality. We have two eyes and can see a narrow band of frequencies we perceive as color as well as the three-dimensional realm where we live. If we had but one eye, we would not have depth perception. Perhaps the more eyes, the more dimensions can be seen, or the more frequencies of colors can be seen. I believe there is much activity going on around each of us that we don't comprehend and is invisible to us.

Thrones and Ophanim

The thrones (Greek *thronos*), or elders, also known as the erelim, or ophanim, are a class of celestial beings mentioned by Paul of Tarsus in Colossians 1:16 (New Testament). They are living symbols of God's justice and authority and have as one of their symbols the throne. These high celestial beings appear to be mentioned again in Revelation 11:16.

The ophanim (Hebrew *ofanim*: wheels, also known as thrones, from the vision of Daniel 7:9) are unusual looking, even compared to the other celestial beings; they appear as a beryl-colored wheel within a wheel, their rims covered with hundreds of eyes.

They are closely connected with the cherubim: "When they moved, the others moved; when they stopped, the others stopped; and when they rose from the earth, the wheels rose along with them; for the spirit of the living creatures [cherubim] was in the wheels" (Ezek. 10:17 NRSV). It looks and sounds like a description of a vehicle or ship to me.

The circle represents two metaphysical truths. First, it traces cycles in history, in which events tend to be repeated on a systematic basis. Second, the relationship between its circumference and its diameter is mathematically irreconcilable (irrational), transcending time-space and pointing toward the infinite. In fact, the circle has long been seen as a symbol of eternity.

The chariot of the Lord included phenomenal living creatures, precious materials, and wheels within wheels. The structure of his celestial transportation vehicle is not incidental. Its myriad rotational interactions are freighted with meaning.

Jewish writings speak of his mind-boggling encounter as *Ma'aseh Merkavah,* or the "account of the chariot." It is of great interest that this same term is used elsewhere by Jewish commentators, who use it to refer to "metaphysical secrets." In other words, the chariot's wheels and rings speak of deeper truths. Their very terminology allows us to see that Ezekiel's wheels reveal the deeper spiritual truths of Scripture. These wheels are described as having "eyes," and their complex interactions are truly inexplicable—i.e., when we understand something, we are said to "see."

Living creatures are also mentioned in God's Word and may be part of the second sphere of heavenly inhabitants.

Second Sphere

Angels of the second sphere work as heavenly governors.

Dominions Hashmalim

The dominions (Latin *dominatio*, plural *dominationes*, also translated from the Greek term *kyriotites* as "lordships") are presented as the hierarchy of celestial beings "lordships" in the *De Coelesti Hierarchia*. The dominions, also known as the *hashmalim*, regulate the duties of lower angels. It is only with extreme rarity that the angelic lords make themselves physically known to humans. They are also the angels who preside over nations.

The dominions are believed to look like divinely beautiful humans with a pair of feathered wings, much like the common representation of angels, but they may be distinguished from other groups by wielding orbs of light fastened to the heads of their scepters or on the pommel of their swords.

Virtues

The virtues or strongholds lie beyond the *ophanim* (thrones/wheels). Their primary duty is to supervise the movements of the heavenly bodies in order to ensure that the cosmos remains in order.

The term appears to be linked to the attribute "might," from the Greek root δύναμις in Ephesians 1:21, which is also translated as "virtue." They are presented as the celestial choir virtues, in the *Summa Theologica*. Traditional theological conceptions of the virtues might appear to describe the same order called the thrones (Greek *thronos*), in which case the ophanim may not be the same thing as thrones (from Dionysius the Areopagite).

Powers or Authorities

The powers (Latin *potestas* [female], plural *potestates*), or authorities, from the Greek *exousies* (see Greek root in Ephesians 3:10) appear to collaborate, in power and authority, with the principalities (rulers).

The powers are the bearers of conscience and the keepers of history. They are also the warrior angels created to be completely loyal to God. Some believe that no power has ever fallen from grace, but another theory states that Satan was the chief of the powers before he fell (see also Ephesians 6:12). Their duty is to oversee the distribution of power among humankind, hence their name.

Third Sphere

Angels who function as heavenly messengers and soldiers.

Principalities or Rulers

The principalities (Latin *principatus*, plural *principatūs*), also translated as "princedoms" and "rulers," from the Greek *arche* (see Greek root in Ephesian 3:10), appear to collaborate, in power and authority, with the powers (authorities).

The principalities are shown wearing a crown and carrying a scepter. Their duty also is said to carry out the orders given to them by the dominions and bequeath blessings to the material world. Their task is to oversee groups of people. They are the educators and guardians of the realm of earth. Like beings related to the world of the *germinal ideas*, they are said to inspire living things to many things, such as art or science.

Paul used the term *rule* and *authority* in Ephesians 1:21, and *rulers* and *authorities* in Ephesians 3:10. He may have been referring to the rulers and authorities of men or societies instead of referring to angels.

Archangels

The word *archangel* comes from the Greek αρχάγγελος (*archangĕlŏs*), meaning *chief angel*, a translation of the Hebrew רב־מלאך (*rav-mal'ákh*). It derives from the Greek *archō*, meaning to be first in rank or power, and *aggĕlŏs*, which means messenger. The word is only used twice in the New Testament, in 1 Thessalonians 4:16 and Jude 1:9. Only the archangel Michael is mentioned by name in the New Testament.

Michael is the only angel the Bible named expressly as *the* archangel. In the book of Daniel, he is referred to as "one of the chief princes." The word *prince* here is the ancient Hebrew word *sar*, which means "a head person (of any rank or class), a chief, a general, etc."

In most Christian traditions, Gabriel is also considered an archangel, but there is no direct literal support for this assumption.

The name of the archangel Raphael appears only in the book of Tobit (Tobias). Tobit is considered deuterocanonical by Roman Catholics (both Eastern and Western rites) and Eastern Orthodox Christians. The book of Tobit is also read by Anglicans and Lutherans, but not by Reformed Christians or Baptists. Raphael said to Tobias that he is "one of the seven who stand before the Lord," and it is generally believed that Michael and Gabriel are two of the other six.

A fourth archangel is Uriel, whose name literally means "fire of God" or "light of God." Uriel's name is the only one not mentioned in the Lutheran Bible, he but plays a prominent role in an apocryphon read by Anglican and Russian Orthodox Christians. The Second Book of Esdras (Fourth Book of Esdras in the Latin Vulgate) unveils seven prophecies to the prophet Ezra, after whom the book is named. He also plays a role in the apocryphal book of Enoch, which is considered canonical only by the Ethiopian Orthodox Church.

Another possible interpretation of the seven archangels is that the seven are the seven spirits of God that stand before the throne described in the book of Enoch and in the book of Revelation.

The seven archangels are said to be the guardian angels of nations and countries and are concerned with the issues and events surrounding these, including politics, military matters, commerce, and trade—e.g., the archangel Michael is traditionally seen as the protector of Israel and of the *ecclesia* (Greek root *ekklesia* from the New Testament passages), theologically equated as the church, the forerunner of the spiritual New Israel.

It is possible to make a distinction between *archangel* (with a lowercase *a*) and *Archangel* (with an uppercase *A*). The former can denote the second-lowest choir (archangels in the sense of being just above the lowest choir of angels that is called only "angels"), but the latter may denote the highest of all the angels (i.e., Archangels in the sense of being above *all* angels, of *any* choir, the seven highest seraphim, Michael being the highest of all, once Satan fell). Most of the angels govern heaven and the cosmos, but Archangels are said to lead the guardian angels of earthly nations and people. These two-winged angels are known as *hashmalim* who deal between God and mankind.

Demons

You don't hear much about demons these days, but Jesus often encountered them and told His disciples about how they behave. Even though we cannot see them, I believe we see the results of their activity every day influencing our families and people around us. The Bible teaches that the shed blood of Jesus cleanses us of sin, and where there is no sin, these demons have no authority and need to be resisted (James). Demons, like cold-blooded serpents, have no stamina and can't sustain an attack long. Therefore, another way to resist them is to ignore them until they tire out. Other ways may be to keep oneself spiritually clean by confessing sin often and taking communion. There is also spiritual protection in Jesus's blood.

Jesus told His disciples how the invisible realm worked in Matthew 12:43–45. This concept of invisible evil spirits or demons entering into people and influencing them is also demonstrated in Mark 5.

The Gerasene Demoniac

> *And they came over unto the other side of the sea, into the country of the Gadarenes. And when he was come out of the ship, immediately there met him out of the tombs a man with an unclean spirit, Who had his dwelling among the tombs; and no man could bind him, no, not with chains: Because that he had been often bound with fetters and chains, and the chains had been plucked asunder by him, and the fetters broken in pieces: neither could any man tame him. And always, night and day, he was in the mountains, and in the tombs, crying, and cutting himself with stones. But when he saw Jesus afar off, he ran and worshipped him, And cried with a loud voice, and said, What have I to do with thee, Jesus, thou Son of the most high God? I adjure thee by God, that thou torment me not. For he said unto him, Come out of the man, thou unclean spirit. And he asked him, What is thy name? And he answered, saying, My name is Legion: for we are many. And he besought him much that he*

would not send them away out of the country. Now there was there nigh unto the mountains a great herd of swine feeding. And all the devils besought him, saying, Send us into the swine, that we may enter into them. And forthwith Jesus gave them leave. And the unclean spirits went out, and entered into the swine: and the herd ran violently down a steep place into the sea, (they were about two thousand;) and were choked in the sea. And they that fed the swine fled, and told it in the city, and in the country. And they went out to see what it was that was done. And they come to Jesus, and see him that was possessed with the devil, and had the legion, sitting, and clothed, and in his right mind: and they were afraid. (Mark 5:1–15 KJV)

When the unclean spirit is gone out of a man, he walketh through dry places, seeking rest, and findeth none. Then he saith, I will return into my house from whence I came out; and when he is come, he findeth it empty, swept, and garnished. Then goeth he, and taketh with himself seven other spirits more wicked than himself, and they enter in and dwell there: and the last state of that man is worse than the first. Even so shall it be also unto this wicked generation. (Matt. 12:43–45 KJV)

Spiritual Warfare

Spiritual warfare exists in the unseen, supernatural dimension, where God is all-powerful and Satan is in revolt. As any Christian soon discovers, although spiritual warfare is unseen, it's absolutely real. The Bible speaks of spiritual warfare in many places, but most directly in Ephesians 6:12, where Paul speaks of putting on the full armor of God:

> *For we wrestle not against flesh and blood,*
> *but against principalities, against powers,*
> *against the rulers of the darkness of this*
> *world, against spiritual wickedness in high*
> *places. (Eph. 6:12 KJV)*

Spiritual warfare is an image that many of us would rather reject. However, since the Bible uses terms of warfare, it's best that we accept God's imagery so that we're properly prepared for real battle. As Christians, we're going through more than a mere "struggle" on earth, and it seems that war imagery captures this reality better than anything else. Since it's warfare, God instructs Christians to use a very specific set of armor and weapons in Ephesians:

> *Stand therefore, having your loins girt*
> *about with truth, and having on the breast-*
> *plate of righteousness; And your feet shod*
> *with the preparation of the gospel of peace;*
> *Above all, taking the shield of faith, where-*
> *with ye shall be able to quench all the fiery*
> *darts of the wicked. And take the helmet of*
> *salvation, and the sword of the Spirit,*
> *which is the Word of God: Praying always*

*with all prayer and supplication in the
Spirit. (Eph. 6:14–18 KJV)*

God's list of weaponry is rather unique—these are
weapons of peace.

Throughout the Bible, you will find examples of God's
weaponry in action. For instance, King Jehoshaphat sent out
praise singers in front of his soldiers to cause disarray among
the enemy, Joshua used singing and trumpets to bring down
the great city of Jericho, and what better example of using
faith in battle than David fighting Goliath with a slingshot?
Of course, the lesson in all these examples (as in all spiritual
warfare today) is that it's only God who allows us to claim
victory over evil!

So, what is the source of demons? In the book of 1
Enoch, the villainous sons of God of Genesis 6:1–4 are not
only called angels; they are called watchers. The link back to
the Mesopotamian giant races of rephaim, anakim, ananke,
and nephilim is unmistakable. The first book of Enoch spells
out how the watchers and their offspring were the source of
demons:

> *And it came to pass, when men began to
> multiply on the face of the earth, and
> daughters were born unto them, ² That the
> sons of God saw the daughters of men that
> they were fair; and they took them wives of
> all which they chose.³ And the LORD said,
> My spirit shall not always strive with man,
> for that he also is flesh: yet his days shall be
> an hundred and twenty years.⁴ There were
> giants in the earth in those days; and also
> after that, when the sons of God came in*

unto the daughters of men, and they bare children to them, the same became mighty men which were of old, men of renown. (Gen. 6:1–4 KJV)

Then Michael, Surafel, and Gabriel observed carefully from the sky and they saw much blood being shed upon the earth, and all the oppression being wrought upon the earth… As for the women, they gave birth to giants to the degree that the whole earth was filled with blood and oppression. And now behold, the Holy One will cry, and those who have died will bring their suit up to the gate of heaven. Their groaning has ascended (into heaven), but they could not get out from before the face of the oppression that is being wrought on earth… And to Gabriel the Lord said, 'Proceed against the bastards and the reprobates and against the children of adultery; and destroy the children of adultery and expel the children of the Watchers from among the people. And send them against one another (so that) they may be destroyed in the fight, for length of days have they not'. And when they and all their children have battled with each other, and when they have seen the destruction of their beloved ones, bind them for 70 generations underneath the rocks of the ground until the day of their judgment and of their consummation, until the eternal judgment is concluded… But now the giants who are

> *born from the (union of) the spirits and the*
> *flesh shall be called evil spirits upon the*
> *earth, because their dwelling shall be upon*
> *the earth and inside the earth. Evil spirits*
> *have come out of their bodies. Because from*
> *the day that they were created from the holy*
> *ones they became the Watchers; their first*
> *origin is the spiritual foundation. They will*
> *become evil upon the earth and shall be*
> *called evil spirits. (1 Enoch 6:1–2, 7:1,*
> *9:1, 9–10, 10:9, 15:8–9)*

(Note: 1 Enoch 6:1–2, 7:1, 9:1, 9:9–10, 10:9, 15:8–9 translation from J. H. Charlesworth, *Old Testament Pseudepigrapha*, vol. 1.)

Ancient Books Shed Some History of Angels and a Broken Heaven

Book of Enoch

The book of Enoch is quoted in the New Testament book of Jude and goes into detail about the fallen angels who left heaven and entered the earth at Mt. Hermon. They swore an oath to corrupt mankind by tampering with mankind's DNA, creating monsters. In this book, Enoch enters a flying house and goes around the world and through time itself. He describes events and places he sees in vivid detail.

Book of Jasher

The book of Jasher is one of thirteen ancient history books that are not contained but are referenced in the Bible (2 Samuel, 2 Timothy). It covers the first 2,516 years of history. It contains the life of Enoch, fallen angels, the death of Nimrod, Abraham, the lives of Jacob, Moses, and Joshua's long day.

Book of Jubilees

The book of Jubilees is found among the Dead Sea Scrolls and in Ethiopia. It contains ancient history repeating the events of Genesis and Exodus with more detail on the fallen angels' and Satan's fall. It divides events in periods of forty-nine years (Jubilees), describing the three types of nephilim and the possible source of demons.

"They started saying to each other, Come, let us select for ourselves wives from the progeny of men and let us beget children" (Gen. 6:1).

The nephilim /ˈnɛfɪˌlɪm/ (Hebrew: נְפִילִים, nefilim) were the offspring of the "sons of God" and the "daughters of men" before the deluge (flood) (Wikipedia).

Anakim (Hebrew: עֲנָקִים ʿĂnāqîm) were described as a race of giants, descended from Anak, according to the Tanakh. They were said to have lived in the southern part of the land of Canaan, near Hebron (Gen. 23:2; Josh. 15:13) (Wikipedia).

In the Hebrew Bible, rephaites, or rephaim, are described as an ancient race of giants in Iron Age Israel. It describes the places where these individuals were thought to have lived. According to Genesis 14:5, King Chedorlaomer and his allies attacked and defeated the rephaites at Ashteroth-Karnaim (Wikipedia).

> *And angels who did not keep their own des-*
> *ignated place of power, but abandoned*
> *their proper dwelling place, [these] He has*
> *kept in eternal chains under [the thick*
> *gloom of utter] darkness for the judgment of*
> *the great day, ⁷ just as Sodom and Gomorrah*
> *and the adjacent cities, since they in the*
> *same way as these angels indulged in gross*
> *immoral freedom and unnatural vice and*
> *sensual perversity. They are exhibited [in*
> *plain sight] as an example in undergoing*
> *the punishment of everlasting fire. (Jude*
> *1:6–7 AMP)*

Many scholars believe that the seed of the woman (human) and the seed of the serpent (evil angel offspring) are at war. The flood wiped out the evil angel offspring that had covered the earth and who made all the megalithic stone structures throughout the world. But through the seed of Ham's wife, it is believed that there was a remnant of the seed that started up after the flood and settled in the Jordan River area in Canaan. Whenever Satan's offspring (these giants) withstood Israel, God always went before them into battle.

The Shining Ones from Ancient Mesopotamia

The early records of these "shining ones" can be found in five basic sources:

1. Sumerian tablets from the library in Nippur, where they are called by the name Anunnaki (Anannage)
2. In the Bible, books of Genesis, Numbers, Deuteronomy, where the name of nephilim was given to them
3. Writings in Greece that can be accounted to Babylonian priest Berossus
4. The book of Enoch, where they are mentioned by the name of angels, watchers, and bephilim
5. The book of Jubilees

Recent Angels Seen in Space

In July of 1984, the Russian *Salyut 7* was on the 155th day of its mission and things were going in a routine fashion until there was a transmission from cosmonauts Commander Oleg Atkov, Vladmir Solovyov, and Leonid Kizim in which they claimed that the space station had been surrounded by a blinding orange light. The crew of three aboard the *Salyut 7* looked out of the portals to try to see what was causing this inexplicable, brilliant glow. At this point they would witness probably the last thing they had expected to see out there.

There hovering in space in front of the space station were what the crew would describe as seven enormous winged humanoid beings estimated as being around ninety feet in height and with calm, smiling faces, and it was from these bizarre entities that the ethereal light was apparently emanating. They were also claimed to exude a feeling of calm and peacefulness, and oddly, the cosmonauts felt no fear during the encounter, merely wonderment. According to the witnesses, the colossal apparitions, which they described as "angels," matched the speed of the space station, remaining in the same position for about ten minutes before fading away. Baffled by what they had all just seen, the three cosmonauts had a heated discussion on what the beings were and what rational explanation could account for it, but they could come up with nothing.

They may have gone on forever convinced that this was some sort of mass hallucination and a bout of temporary insanity, but it would not be their last encounter with these otherworldly beings. On day 167 of the mission, the *Salyut* gained an additional three cosmonauts, Svetlana Savitskaya, Igor Volk, and Vladimir Dzhanibekov. Not long after these new crew members boarded, the station was once again bathed in that bright orange light, and this time all six of the crew looked out of the portholes to see several of the massive angelic beings in the blackness of space outside, again with their benevolent, smiling faces. Considering that this time they had again all seen the same thing, it appeared that there was perhaps something more going on beyond simple hallucinations.

Fallen Angels

> *It happened after the sons of men had multiplied in those days that daughters were born to them, elegant and beautiful. And when the angels, the sons of heaven, beheld them, they became enamored of them. They started saying to each other, Come, let us select for ourselves wives from the progeny of men and let us beget children. (Gen. 6:1–4 KJV)*

The earliest account of the beings mentioned above can be found on Sumerian tablets. Sumerians invented writing, and they also had advanced knowledge of music, poetry, art, mathematics, astronomy, and science. For ancient Sumerians, music was the tool that helped them to describe the universe.

- Fallen angels are angels who were expelled from heaven. In the Abrahamic religions, they are former agents of God and the enemies of humanity. The term *fallen angel* appears neither in the Bible nor in Islamic scriptures but is used of angels who were cast out of heaven or angels who sinned, such as those referred to in 2 Peter 2:4 (KJV), "For if God did not spare angels when they sinned, but cast them into hell and committed them to chains of gloomy darkness to be kept until the judgment."
- Noah was found pure in his generations, but his son's wives may not have been pure, and this seed traversed the flood, resulting in the giants like Goliath and the nephilim. Angel worship became prevalent.

This truncated list is taken from many sources and may not be accurate but gives an element of truth to the extent of angelic rebellion against God.

Some Names of the Fallen Angels

- Abaddon—fallen angel of death, whose name means "to destroy"
- Abezethibou—one-winged Red Sea fallen angel
- Allocen—fallen angel who is a duke in hell.

- Amduscias—name of the fallen angel who appears as a unicorn
- Amon—fallen angel who is a strong marquis over forty legions (240,000)
- Andras—fallen angel marquis and appears raven-headed
- Andrealphus—fallen angel who can transform humans into birds
- Andromalius—fallen angel who appears as a man holding a serpent
- Apollyon—fallen angel of death; same as Abaddon
- Armaros—fallen angel who teaches the "resolving of enchantments"
- Asmoday—fallen angel king with three heads: a bull, a ram, and a man
- Asmodeus—one of the evilest of fallen angels, being an archdemon
- Azael—evil, fallen angel who cohabited with women
- Azazel—fallen angel whose name means "God strengthens"
- Azza—fallen angel whose name means "the strong"
- Baal—fallen angel whose name means "the Lord"
- Balberith—fallen angel who is a grand pontiff in hell
- Baraqijal—fallen angel who teaches astrology
- Barbatos—fallen angel who is a great count, earl, and duke of hell
- Bathin—fallen angel who rides a pale horse
- Beelzebub—fallen angel known as the "prince of demons"
- Satan—Christian fallen angel whose name means "adversary"

- Seere—fallen angel who appears as a man on a winged horse
- Semyaza—fallen angel leader

The word *angel* in the Greek means "messenger" or "one sent forth." *Evangelist* contains the word *angel* and means "one sent forth by God to spread the good news of the gospel." Jesus said that the righteous shall live by faith, do the works that He does, and that God gives them the power to become sons of God. Paul said, "Don't you know that your bodies are the temple of the Holy Spirit?" It would seem that a person that is "born again" and Spirit filled may become an angel of God, a messenger that spreads the gospel.

Are Crop Circles a Form of Angelic Communication?

Mention crop circles and many will laugh or roll their eyes. Most think of England as the "crop circle center" of the world, but crop circles have been documented in many other countries as well, not just in England. Even in the arctic snow. It is true that about 90 percent of crop circles are found in Southern England. The phenomena of crop circles have been around at least since the seventeenth century. In 1678, a "mowing devil" photo showed up in a newspaper, showing a devil-like person cutting a circle into a field.

Some believe that the spiral depictions and swirls shown on cave drawings and wall carvings from ancient civilizations are actually depicting crop circles. If so, is this their way of telling us that a crop circle was formed there or had been seen by many? Basketball-size balls of light accompany many crop circle formations. It is interesting that the rank of angels known as dominions, or *hashmalim*, which are set over countries, often are depicted with orbs of light dangling from their spears or swords. In just a few seconds, small orbs of light the size of a basketball zip through a field of grain and etch out beautiful geometric forms. Where do these balls of light come from? Maybe from another dimension or heaven. They are seen traveling at very high speeds and turning on a dime that would be fatal for earthbound life. An explanation perhaps is other dimensional ability, such as an angel that is not governed by earthly laws of gravity or momentum. The angel over England seems to be very active in their crop fields. There is so much we don't know. Jesus said He came so that mankind could have a more abundant life, and He taught about the kingdom of God everywhere He went. He demonstrated how to operate in this invisible realm by doing miracles that went against our laws of nature.

Crop circles come in many shapes and sizes. Some have been as large as two hundred thousand square feet! That's some feat! As the history of crop circles evolved, even more intricate designs have appeared. The first crop circles were mostly simple circles and crosses. Then the designs became more complex and larger. They remind me of snowflakes, where infinite numbers exist but are all different. Each snowflake is a beautiful geometric design with perfect symmetry, not an ugly, distorted flake among them.

Conclusion

In this chapter we have examined who God is by looking at God's creation of the heavens and earth. Even the stars of the heavens tell the gospel story of God's plan for mankind's ascension to heaven. We examined the lower dimensional realms to get an idea of what heaven may be like. We saw a glimpse of the design of God's creation by looking at numbers in the Bible, and we looked at the angelic creation to see the complexity of God's heavenly operations.

The heavens are telling the glory of God; they are a marvelous display of his crafts- manship. Day and night they keep on tell- ing about God. (Ps. 19:1–2 KJV)

In the next chapter we will look at God's creation of mankind and see why the fig leaves were not good enough to cover Adam and Eve in the garden of Eden, why Cain's sacri- fice from his garden was not acceptable, and why a virgin birth of Jesus was necessary.

CHAPTER 3

Who Is Mankind?

God said, "Let's make man in our image."
After God created the earth, He planted a garden and put the tree of life in the center. And next to it He put the tree of the knowledge of good and evil. In the center position of the garden, He put the tree of life, showing it is the central theme of God's plan. The tree of life represents eternal life for mankind and relationship with God. In Genesis 3:22, He makes known His plan to make man in His own image. The Triune God created mankind in His own image with three parts, a body, a soul, and a spirit. Interestingly, there is no mention of God creating angels or animals in His image. He formed man's body from the dust of the earth and then breathed his breath of life into man. This breath of God may represent man's spirit that can have relationship with God, who is Spirit. When mankind sinned, relationship with God was broken, indicating that mankind's spirit became broken and death entered the earthly realm. Death in the biblical sense means separation from God. So man became like God, knowing good and evil, but gradually chose evil with a little help from some evil angels. After the flood, God chose Abraham to start man's restoration back to fellowship.

God reveals Himself to mankind through the fall into sin, and the struggles in life teach us of His truths. God cursed Satan and the ground, but not mankind. He promised a Savior would come, and the Old Testament of the Bible gives over 330 prophecies concerning Christ's first coming, and there are over 600 prophecies of His second coming. God's plans for mankind's salvation are outlined in chapter 4 of this book, but let's look first at the meaning of changing Abraham's and Sarah's names.

An Example of the Neshamah Being Restored

The breath of God (*neshamah* in Hebrew) is represented by the *H* sound. An interesting thing happened when God came to Abram and opened communication with him. Abram's name was changed to Abra*h*am (Gen. 17:5), and Sarai's name was changed to Sara*h* by God (Gen. 17:15). I believe when communication/relationship was restored, God restored their broken spirit so that they could be in covenant with Him. God added an *H* to their names, showing that they had become different people (born again of the Spirit).

The breath of God is sometimes represented by the *H* (fifth Hebrew letter He or Hay, ה) together with the Hebrew letter *yod* (our English *y* and or *J*) also represents God Himself (pronounced "JH" or "Ja"). The numerical value of the two letters together is 15, a holy number in some Jewish circles.

The Spoken Word has breath and is able to restore mankind back to God. We believe with our heart and confess with our mouth for salvation.

Jesus's main teaching while here on earth was about the kingdom of God or the kingdom of heaven. He taught that sin separated us from God and changed mankind to a fallen state, but He was the answer to the sin problem. He came to save, restore, and prepare mankind for heaven. Once saved, we become a new creation in Christ and start living spiritually in His kingdom. Reading the Word daily introduces us to God, gives us wisdom to renew our minds, and gives direction to walk through life according to the calling we have received. Jesus gave many examples of what the kingdom of God is like. He did this by teaching parallel truths or parables and by doing what the Father told Him to do on earth. Jesus breathed on the disciples to receive the Holy Spirit and restore their broken spirit, "breath of God." All we have to do for salvation is believe the gospel with our hearts and confess with our mouths. Our words come from our hearts (spirit), not our minds, showing proof that we believe. Knowing about the gospel isn't enough. We need to believe in our hearts and learn to "say" what we believe (Ps. 91:2, 107:2, 122:8; Prov. 18:21). Action and/or confession is part of believing.

> *Death and life are in the power of the tongue: and they that love it shall eat the fruit thereof. (Prov. 18:21 KJV)*

> *The word is nigh thee, even in thy mouth, and in thy heart: that is, the word of faith, which we preach; That if thou shalt confess with thy mouth the Lord Jesus, and shalt believe in thine heart that God hath raised him from the dead, thou shalt be saved. For with the heart man believeth unto righteousness; and with the mouth confession is made unto salvation. (Rom. 10:8–10 KJV)*

Whosoever therefore shall confess me before men, him will I confess also before my Father which is in heaven. But whosoever shall deny me before men, him will I also deny before my Father which is in heaven. (Matt. 10:32–33 KJV)

The Three Battlefields

In the beginning, God made mankind in His image (Gen. 1:26 KJV) and gave him dominion (authority) over the earth to subdue it.

I believe our flesh has a voice for earthly things, our soul (subconscious mind) has a voice to relate to others, and our spirit has a voice to relate to God. The three work together and make us who we are. We are made in the image of God, and He created the universe by speaking. Since God is Spirit, we need to address God in spirit. We need to learn to use the voice of our spirit. James said we have not because we ask not. To help do this, start with hope, move to imagination, and visualize what we are asking (praying about) to be completed, then finally thank God for it, which shows faith.

Man fights against evil on three battlefields, his own flesh, the world, and the demonic realm.

God has provided weapons for each battlefield. We are to crucify our fleshly lusts (selfishness), cast out demons in the name of Jesus, and use the blood of Jesus on sin. You cannot cast out flesh or crucify demons. In our fallen state, we didn't have to learn to be bad; it just became natural. So also, when we receive the Holy Spirit and are born of the spirit, it becomes natural to be holy and good in our spirit. Jesus told Nicodemus that a person can't see or even enter the kingdom of God until they are born again. But we still must contend with our selfish flesh and our soul.

> *Among whom also we all had our conversation in times past in the lusts of our flesh, fulfilling the desires of the flesh and of the mind; and were by nature the children of wrath, even as others. (Eph. 2:3 KJV)*

> *For all that is in the world, the lust of the flesh, and the lust of the eyes, and the pride of life, is not of the Father, but is of the world. (1 John 2:16 KJV)*

> *Verily, verily, I say unto thee, Except a man be born again, he cannot see the kingdom of God. (John 3:3 KJV)*

> *For we wrestle not against flesh and blood, but against principalities, against powers, against the rulers of the darkness of this world, against spiritual wickedness in high places. (Eph. 6:12 KJV)*

> *This I say therefore, and testify in the Lord, that ye henceforth walk not as other Gentiles walk, in the vanity of their mind, 18 Having the understanding darkened, being alienated from the life of God through the ignorance that is in them, because of the blindness of their heart. (Eph. 4:18 KJV)*

And these signs shall follow them that believe; In my name shall they cast out devils; they shall speak with new tongues. (Mark 16:17 KJV)

And whatsoever ye shall ask in my name, that will I do, that the Father may be glorified in the Son. If ye shall ask any thing in my name, I will do it. (John 14:13 KJV)

Mankind fights on three levels: (1) think (soul), (2) say (spirit), and (3) do (flesh). The law is based on what we do, but grace is based on what we say.

Man sinned in body, soul, and spirit:

And when the woman saw that the tree was good for food [body] and that it was pleasant to the eyes, [soul] and a tree to be desired to make one wise [spirit)], she took of the fruit thereof, and did eat. (Gen. 3:6 KJV)

For all that is in the world, the lust of the flesh, and the lust of the eyes, and the pride of life, is not of the Father, but is of the world. (1 John 2:16 KJV)

Fallen Man in Need of Salvation

For the life of the flesh is in the blood: and I have given it to you upon the altar to make an atonement for your souls: for it is the blood that maketh an atonement for the soul. (Lev. 17:11 KJV)

Only be sure that thou eat not the blood: for the blood is the life; and thou mayest not eat the life with the flesh. (Deut. 12:23 KJV)

When Adam and Eve sinned in the garden of Eden, they found themselves naked and tried to cover themselves with fig leaves. The fig leaves only covered their physical nakedness, and they lost sight of their spiritual side. Their sin separated them from God, who is Spirit. The all-knowing God knew this would happen and provided a way back through a future event where He Himself (in the form of His Word, Jesus) would become a man and pay the price for all sin through the shedding of His holy, innocent blood. Holy blood became the shadow of an event yet to come that would bring mankind back to God. God started teaching man about His plan of salvation when He exchanged the fig leaves for bloody animal skins in Eden. He killed an innocent animal and put the bloody skins on Adam and Eve to cover both their physical and spiritual nakedness. Cain refused to use the blood covering for sin and gave an offering from his garden. Without the shedding of blood, there is no covering of sin. God warned Cain to do what is right (blood sacrifice) and his sacrifice would be accepted; if not, sin was at the door. Cain became jealous of Abel, refused to offer the blood sacrifice, was tempted, killed his brother Abel, and was marked for separation from God.

The Saving Blood of Jesus

The physical characteristics of blood and the function of blood in our physical body provide a spiritual parallel and insight to the understanding of the significance of Christ's shed blood for the world.

Blood is made up of three main parts, plasma, cells, and clotting agents.

Blood is a connective tissue that flows continually to all parts of the body, bringing life-giving nutrients and carrying away waste just as the blood of Christ connects us with the kingdom of God and carries away sin. Where the blood does not reach, death occurs. The body lives where blood flows. Those that reject God's plan for salvation through the blood of Jesus shed on the cross will not receive everlasting life.

The blood cells are of two types, red for nourishment, and white for protection, just as the shed blood of Jesus brings provision and protection to God's family. The blood continually carries away waste products from the natural body, and Christ's blood covers (carries away) sin in each saint in their past, present, and future. Blood clots around a wound to promote healing as Holy Spirit and the saints gather around the sick to promote their healing.

Scientists have found that the father of a child determines the blood type. Jesus had His Father's blood type! He was God and man able to bridge the gap between heaven and earth for mankind.

The life is in the blood according to God and is sacred:

> For the life of the flesh is in the blood: and I have given it to you upon the altar to make an atonement for your souls: for it is the blood that maketh an atonement for the

> *soul. Therefore I said unto the children of*
> *Israel, No soul of you shall eat blood, nei-*
> *ther shall any stranger that sojourneth*
> *among you eat blood. (Lev. 17:11–12 KJV)*

As a shadow of Christ's shed blood, animal's blood is sacred and should be covered with dust when spilled on the ground:

> *And whatsoever man there be of the chil-*
> *dren of Israel, or of the strangers that sojourn*
> *among you, which hunteth and catcheth*
> *any beast or fowl that may be eaten; he shall*
> *even pour out the blood thereof, and cover it*
> *with dust. (Lev. 17:13 KJV)*

Man's blood is sacred because man was made in God's image:

> *But flesh with the life thereof, which is the*
> *blood thereof, shall ye not eat. And surely*
> *your blood of your lives will I require; at the*
> *hand of every beast will I require it, and at*
> *the hand of man; at the hand of every man's*
> *brother will I require the life of man. Whoso*
> *sheddeth man's blood, by man shall his*
> *blood be shed: for in the image of God made*
> *he man. (Gen. 9:4–6 KJV)*

The shedding of man's blood is particularly sinful as it is an act of usurping the authority of God. Only God gives and takes life. Thus, to take a life borders on idolatry by placing your authority above God's.

Jesus poured out His blood for mankind in three places, Gethsemane, Gabbatha, and Golgotha, to clean man in body, soul, and spirit.

At Gethsemane, Jesus suffered vicarious mental and emotional agony in His soul:

> *Then cometh Jesus with them unto a place called Gethsemane, and saith unto the disciples, Sit ye here, while I go and pray yonder. And he took with him Peter and the two sons of Zebedee, and began to be sorrowful and very heavy. Then saith he unto them, My **soul** is exceeding sorrowful, even unto death: tarry ye here, and watch with me. (Matt. 26:36–38 KJV)*

> *And there appeared an angel unto him from heaven, strengthening him. And being in an agony he prayed more earnestly: and his sweat was as it were great drops of blood falling down to the ground. (Luke 22:43–44 KJV)*

At Gabbatha, Jesus suffered vicariously in His **body** for our health. By His stripes we are healed.

At the pavement (Gabbatha) in front of the Roman courts of Pilate, Jesus was mocked and whipped with a multilashed instrument that had metal tips on each lash, and received the crown of thorns upon His head. Thorns may represent the curse on the ground that occurred when Adam sinned in the garden, now mended.

> *When Pilate therefore heard that saying, he brought Jesus forth, and sat down in the*

judgment seat in a place that is called the Pavement, but in the Hebrew, Gabbatha. (John 19:13 KJV)

Then released he Barabbas unto them: and when he had scourged Jesus, he delivered him to be crucified. (Matt. 27:26 KJV)

Bar means "son," and *abbas* means "father," so *Barabbas* means "son of the father." Jesus was the Son of the Father too. Two identical people standing before Pilate, one killed and one let go. Sounds like the fulfillment of the scapegoat ceremony prophecy.

Then Pilate therefore took Jesus, and scourged him. And the soldiers plaited a crown of thorns, and put it on his head, and they put on him a purple robe, And said, Hail, King of the Jews! and they smote him with their hands. (John 19:1–3 KJV)

The plowers plowed upon my back: they made long their furrows. (Ps. 129:3 KJV)

I gave my back to the smiters, and my cheeks to them that plucked off the hair: I hid not my face from shame and spitting. (Isa. 50:6 KJV)

At Golgotha, Jesus was nailed to the cross by His hands and feet. His side was slashed open with a spear, and water and blood gushed out. He bled and died for our **spiritual** rebirth.

Attributes and Pitfalls

In the kingdom of God, humility is considered strength, mercy rejoices over judgment, and a person does not force his will over someone else's will but seeks agreement through love and fellowship. Mankind should seek unity with others as much as possible because God has given mankind free will and dominion here on earth. God does not force His will but consults His prophets for agreement (Amos 3:7). The Holy Spirit is sensitive to this rule and, when resisted, often just leaves. He needs to be invited to operate according to kingdom rules.

Romans 14:17 (KJV) describes the kingdom attributes in a few words. "For the kingdom of God is not meat and drink, but righteousness, and peace, and joy, in the Holy Spirit." By these marks and attributes, this kingdom is known and distinguished from all others.

In Hebrews chapters 3 and 4, we are warned four times about getting a hard heart toward the things of God. We do this by getting caught up in worldly pleasures, staying away from other saints or church, and not spending time reading the Bible. These things cause us to drift away from God sometimes without even knowing it. We need to keep on spending time with God to show Him we trust Him in the affairs of our life.

Salvation is like driving a car.

God's plan of salvation makes no sense when it is observed from a distance, just like a person who had never seen a car would not be able to perceive functionality or purpose just by looking at one for the first time. To him a boat anchor would have more use. But if he opened the door and sat in the car, saw all the buttons and knobs, and heard that it could move a person from one place to another, he might investigate further, just like a new Christian may start getting interested in God's plan of salvation when he learns that it may affect his eternal destination.

The first step to get a car moving is to read the instructions on how to start the car, and the first step toward understanding salvation is to read God's instruction book, which He has provided, "Basic Instruction Book Before Leaving Earth" (Bible). The second step in driving a car is to put the car in drive, and a new Christian must start believing what God says is true about salvation. Believing what God says is true and acting on those beliefs starts things moving. Thirdly, we have to avoid hitting something and wrecking the car. We have to learn to steer around obstacles, and a new Christian must avoid unforgiveness, fear, gossip, foul language, drugs, etc. and obey the road signs. Stop when you come to a stop sign, yield when you come to a yield sign, and don't look in the rearview mirror while trying to drive forward. Looking in the rearview mirror is like looking at past mistakes and will only distract you. Learn to compromise for the sake of peace and don't worry about what other people are not doing. Only God can fix them. A parked car will not respond to steering, braking, or acceleration commands. The car must be moving. Likewise, a Christian must be actively trying to live a godly life in order to hear which way to go. Always reaching forward by faith and not looking back, we learn to hear the guidance commands. Stay engaged and God will lead you.

The car won't go far without fuel. It provides the power to move the car along. A Christian also needs power to overcome the steep hills of life. God provides a helper (the Holy Spirit) to guide us along life's pathways and point us in the right direction. It is not by our abilities, but by His Spirit, says the Lord.

We see and understand spiritual things through our restored spirit, not through mental reasoning or experience, and our minds are renewed slowly as we are exposed to the truth of God's Word.

> *And be not conformed to this world: but be ye transformed by the renewing of your mind, that ye may prove what is that good, and acceptable, and perfect, will of God. (Rom. 12:2 KJV)*

> *But the natural man receiveth not the things of the Spirit of God: for they are foolishness unto him: neither can he know them, because they are spiritually discerned. (1 Cor. 2:14 KJV)*

Jesus demonstrated resurrection from the dead.

Jesus is called the firstfruits because He was the first person who was raised from the dead with a new, resurrected body, like we will have when we are raised from the dead. Others were brought back to life, but they didn't have a resurrected body. They were put back into their corruptible old bodies. What is amazing is that maybe God took a picture of Jesus's resurrection! Before photography was invented, God might have created a negative on the burial cloth of Jesus during transformation. It was neatly folded and left in the tomb.

The Shroud of Turin is a fourteen-foot-long linen cloth bearing the negative image of a crucified man with wounds matching those on Jesus at His death. The man was laid on one end of the cloth, facing up, and the other end was put over His face. The photographic images of both his front and back are etched into the cloth using unknown energy with three-dimensional accuracy that can be reconstructed using today's technology. This controversial cloth has been analyzed several times for authenticity, even down to the microscopic pollen and weaving of the cloth.

It was first reported in France during the 1350s, moved to Italy about 1418, back to the house of Savoy in France, and then to the Cathedral of St. John in Turin, Italy. Crop circles, Noah's ark, and now the Shroud of Turin are physical evidence that the Bible is true.

Conclusion

We see that God made mankind a trinity with a body to relate to the earthly realm, spirit to relate to God, and the heavenly realm and a soul to relate to one another. Mankind sinned in body, soul, and spirit. We examined the results of sin, where our spirit became broken and death entered our reality. We learned about the work of Jesus that offers forgiveness of sin for those who understand the truth about sin and repent. Last, we examined some of the mysteries and the attributes of salvation. Mankind fights on three battlefields, His own flesh, the world system, and the unseen demonic realm. God has provided weapons for each battlefield. We are to crucify our fleshly desires, cast out demons in the name of Jesus, and apply the blood of Christ on sin. You cannot cast out flesh or crucify demons. We are made in the image of God and are able to become holy and fellowship with Him through our regenerated spirit. Our spirit is infinite in nature and gives us the ability to see the kingdom of God. We, like snowflakes, are as numerous as the sands of the sea, each one geometrically beautiful in God's eyes, who does not desire any to perish.

In the next chapter we will investigate the plans of God for us and some of His life processes. Looking at Bible stories, symbology, parables of Jesus, and His teachings, we will glean more truth from God's perspective.

CHAPTER 4

God's Plans

God's plan is to redeem both heaven and earth,
according to Colossians 1:20. Not much is said
about the angels who rebelled in heaven or their
process of redemption, but here on earth God's plans of salvation includes everybody, both Jew and Gentile. A redeemer
was promised that would solve the sin problem and reunite
God and mankind. The plan for reconciling the earth is
repeated over and over in the Bible stories and Bible symbology. This story is called the good news or the gospel.

God's Plan Is Salvation for Mankind

Salvation is a free gift from God and is received when
we believe in Jesus and the work He did on the cross. Through
one man (Adam) sin came into the world, and through one
man (Jesus) salvation comes to us. It occurs when we seek
His righteousness, not our own. There is nothing we can do
in our own strength to gain eternal life. God offers the gift of
salvation to everyone, but each individual needs to receive it.
After we are saved, we begin a process of sanctification where
God starts making us fit for heaven. We become (sacred)

holy (separated to God) and justified (Rom. 3:24). Salvation comes by believing what Jesus has done and not by being a good person, as the enemy would like us to believe (Rom. 1:16). By knowing and accepting God's promises and accepting the vicarious work of Jesus, we are saved. God, then, is free to change our hearts from a stony one to a good one and moves into our hearts. We are sealed with His Holy Spirit to help us through life, and we become born again into the family of God. Repentance is a continuous process that can occur before, during, or after salvation, where we change our thinking from worldly, carnal-centered concepts to heavenly, spiritually centered concepts. As we read the Bible truths and see things through God's eyes, we are changed into the image of Christ (James 1:23). Our brains get rewired or polarized on godly principles. Salvation also covers all our needs through faith in every part of our lives, spiritual, emotional, social, mental, physical, financial, and material. With our refurbished spirit we can pull these things from the heavenly realm. Though we are earthly bound physically, we are seated in heaven spiritually. Salvation usually starts with a desire to get right with God. As we cry out to God with our whole heart, He hears our prayer and saves us. God supplies faith to believe that He is real, and He rewards those who diligently seek Him.

Jesus's main teaching while here on earth was about the kingdom of God or the kingdom of heaven. He taught that sin separated us from God and changed mankind to a fallen state, but He was the answer to the sin problem. He came to save and restore mankind. Once saved, we become a new creation in Christ and start living in His kingdom. God gives us the gift of His Holy Spirit to help and guide each of us. It is God's job to make us wholly separated for good works. We develop a hunger for the Word of God, reading it daily to renew our minds and walk through life according to the calling we have received. Jesus gave many examples of what the kingdom of God is like. He did this in parables and in His actions while on earth.

God's plan is to work through contracts or covenants with mankind to guide us into salvation.

God doesn't change, but He has dealt with sin differently at different times. Before the law was given, He often did not impute sin to a person (Rom. 5:13, James 2:23). When Jesus was on the cross, He said, "Forgive them for they know not what they are doing." After the law was given by Moses, God became very strict in order to stem the rampant growth of sin. People became afraid of the consequences of sin. The laws of God revealed sin. After Jesus completed His work of salvation and mankind was under grace, God put the law into our hearts and renewed a right spirit within us to help us resist sin.

The Sanctification Process

It is God's plan to make us ready for heaven while still here on earth. Many people don't understand that when they accept Jesus as their Lord and Savior, spiritually they move from an earthly dwelling to a heavenly dwelling. Eternity starts for the believer when becoming a Christian, and God starts teaching new converts the rules of heaven.

We see this sanctification pattern when God delivered Israel from the taskmasters of Egypt. God told Israel that He was giving them a new land that flowed with milk and honey. But when the ten spies were sent into the promised land, they didn't believe God, and all the spies, except Caleb and Joshua, came back full of fear, doubt, and unbelief, which is incompatible with heavenly living. Everyone in heaven believes that God's Word is true, because God can't lie. Jesus demonstrated the same principle when crossing the sea of Galilee with His disciples. He told them that they were crossing to the other side, but when the storm came, they didn't believe His words and relied on worldly circumstances around them. The first lesson Christians learn is to believe and trust God. That's why we are called "believers." The just shall live by faith!

Many bad things started happening as the Hebrews traveled to the promised land. They depended on themselves and their experience and didn't trust God. They grumbled and complained instead of asking for what they needed. They were self-centered, full of pride, but at the same time, good things happened too:

> *He brought them forth also with silver and gold: and [there was] not one feeble [person] among their tribes. (Ps. 105:37 KJV)*

> *And I have led you forty years in the wilderness: your clothes are not waxen old upon you, and thy shoe is not waxen old upon thy foot. (Deut. 29:5 KJV)*

> *Yea, forty years didst thou sustain them in the wilderness, [so that] they lacked nothing; their clothes waxed not old, and their feet swelled not. (Neh. 9:21 KJV)*

God took good care of the Hebrews and gave them everything they needed for forty years as they wandered through the deserts of Sinai. They learned to trust and believe God.

Manna

Manna was the bread of life that came down from heaven. Physically, it was a round white coriander-like seed that could be made into flour for baking bread, and it fed each person for the forty years as they wandered through the desert. Spiritually, it was a symbol of Jesus coming down from heaven and providing eternal life for mankind. It had a short shelf life and had to be consumed that day or it would spoil. This speaks of a daily routine of feeding on God's spiritual food for a forty-year lifetime. We are to live one day at a time.

> And he humbled thee, and suffered thee to hunger, and fed thee with manna, which thou knewest not, neither did thy fathers know; that he might make thee know that man doth not live by bread only, but by every [word] that proceedeth out of the mouth of the LORD doth man live. (Deut. 8:3 KJV)

> And when the dew that lay was gone up, behold, upon the face of the wilderness [there lay] a small round thing, [as] small as the hoar frost on the ground. And when the children of Israel saw [it], they said one to another, It [is] manna: for they wist not what it [was]. And Moses said unto them,

This [is] the bread which the LORD hath given you to eat. (Exod. 16:14–15 KJV)

And the house of Israel called the name thereof Manna: and it [was] like coriander seed, white; and the taste of it [was] like wafers [made] with honey. (Exod. 16:31 KJV)

Manna is a symbol of Jesus (the bread of life) and represents what He has done for us and the provision that is available for us through faith (John 6:41–50; 1 Cor. 10:16–17; Rev. 2:17).

The next time you go to the grocery store, go to the spice section and examine the coriander seed spice. Notice the scars, scratches, and bumps on each seed. I believe they represent the knocks of life that Jesus suffered for us and what we, too, go through preparing us for kingdom living in heaven.

Throughout history, God has slowly developed mankind through covenants or contracts.

Adamic Covenant

Covenant theology first sees a covenant of works administered with Adam in the garden of Eden. Upon Adam's failure, God established the covenant of grace in the promised seed of the woman (Gen. 3:15).

The Adamic covenant is declared in Genesis 3:14–19 as a result of Adam and Eve's sin. This is known as the "fall of mankind," since Adam and Eve's disobedience to God resulted in the legacy of a sin nature in all generations thereafter.

When these first humans were placed in the garden of Eden, they had all they would ever need. It was beautiful, food was plentiful, and there was no need for anything else. The only restriction issued to them was to not eat from the tree in the middle of the garden. The serpent (Satan's disguise) tempted the woman, and she was deceived to eat of the tree's forbidden fruit. She then took the fruit to Adam, who willingly ate the fruit he knew was prohibited.

Most people are familiar with this account, but few realize the consequences brought upon the entire human race thereafter. God had told the couple in verses 3 and 4 that if they ate of it, they would die (Gen. 3:3). Defying God is sin, and without seeking His forgiveness, our relationship with God is severed. The warning of death was about an impending eternal, spiritual death. God issued a curse against the serpent and the land and a judgment against the woman and the man as a result.

The Curse and Judgment

The effect of disobedience by Adam and Eve in the garden was the legacy left to all mankind. Genesis 3:14–15 states, "So the Lord God said to the serpent, 'Because you have done this, cursed are you above all the livestock and all the wild animals! You will crawl on your belly and you will eat dust all the days of your life. [Hmmm, did the serpent have legs and walk like a dinosaur?] And I will put enmity between you and the woman, and between your offspring and hers; he will crush your head, and you will strike [bruise] his heel."

When God said the offspring of woman would crush the head of the enemy and would merely have a bruised heel, it was used to symbolize the promise of victory through Jesus over Satan (Rom. 16:20).

In Genesis 3:17, God said to Adam, "Cursed is the ground because of you; through painful toil you will eat of it all the days of your life. It will produce thorns and thistles for you, and you will eat the plants of the field. By the sweat of your brow you will eat your food until you return to the ground, since from it you were taken; for dust you are and to dust you will return."

These words were the punishment for man to labor all his days in order to eat. Adam and Eve were cast from the garden of Eden, where they had been handed everything without having to work for it. Their sin changed all that. They would never have known of evil or death had they not disobeyed God. But God would provide a way for them to be reconciled through sacrifice.

The Redemption

Redemption was secured in the Adamic covenant when God cursed the serpent. The curses are inescapable, but a great promise of grace and forgiveness was issued. It was not wrong for Adam and Eve to want to be "godlike," that is, to mirror His characteristics, and that is a good and worthy goal. But to want to become God and take His place is rebellion against God. We would be attempting to place ourselves above Him. Beware of Satan's deceit and lies. God is supreme and sovereign and cannot be outdone.

God said the serpent would be at enmity with the seed of the woman and his head would be crushed. Here God promises that the "seed" of a woman would defeat Satan; that seed is

Jesus Christ (Gal. 4:4, 1 John 3:8). In the middle of the curse, God's gracious gift for redemption through Jesus is given.

Noahic Covenant

The Noahic covenant is found in Genesis 8:20–9:17.

The Noahic covenant begins with the circumstances of Genesis 6 and is the result of man's wickedness. In the first seventeen verses we hear that man's evil thoughts and wicked behaviors grieved God and filled His heart with pain. His beloved children totally rejected Him and became putrid and vile. But verse 8 says only Noah found favor with God because he was a righteous man.

Since the people of the earth were unbearably corrupt and violent, God intended to put an end to it by destroying all people and His creation, earth. However, since Noah was a good and righteous man, God tells him in verse 14 to build an ark of cypress wood with exact specifications.

The need for this huge vessel is found in verses 17–18, when God explains and makes His covenant with Noah: "I am going to bring floodwaters on the earth to destroy all life under the heavens, every creature that has the breath of life in it. Everything on earth will perish. But I will establish my covenant with you and you will enter the ark—you and your sons and your wife and your son's wives with you." In the rest of the chapter, God instructs Noah to gather two of all living creatures, food to sustain themselves and all the creatures, as well as more food to be stored. Noah obeyed; the great flood was coming, and when it was time, God told Noah to board the ark with his family.

God made the Noahic covenant as a pledge to replenish the earth with those on board the ark. The importance of God's divine promise is reaffirmed to Noah and his sons:

> *Then God said to Noah and to his sons with him: "I now establish my covenant with you and with your descendants after you and with every living creature that was with you—the birds, the livestock and all the wild animals, all those that came out of the ark with you—every living creature on earth. I establish my covenant with you: Never again will all life be cut off by the waters of a flood; never again will there be a flood to destroy the earth." (Gen. 9:8–11)*

> *And God said, "This is the sign of the covenant I am making between me and you and every living creature with you, a covenant for all generations to come: I have set my rainbow in the clouds, and it will be the sign of the covenant between me and the earth." (Gen. 9:12–13)*

This covenant demonstrated God's infinite mercy to all who are holy and obedient to Him. It was through Noah and his family that all humankind is descended. By the promise to Noah, we see the rainbows as reminders that we, too, have the offer of God's mercy.

As the Noahic covenant illustrates, God is unwilling to let sinfulness and corrupt disobedience of man to continue forever. He promised to never again destroy the earth by flood, but He will not allow our iniquity to continue. The next judgment of the world's iniquities will be by a different means, but there will be judgment.

> *The Lord is not slow in keeping his promise, as some understand slowness. He is patient with you, not wanting anyone to perish, but everyone to come to repentance. But the day of the Lord will come like a thief. The heavens will disappear with a roar; the elements will be destroyed by fire, and the earth and everything in it will be laid bare. (2 Pet. 3:9–10)*

Abrahamic Covenant

The Abrahamic covenant is found in Genesis chapters 12, 15, and 17.

In contrast with the covenants made with Adam or Noah, which were universal in scope, this covenant was with a particular people. Abraham is promised a seed and a land, although he would not see its fruition within his own lifetime. The book of Hebrews explains that he was looking to a better and heavenly land, a city with foundations, whose builder and architect is God (11:8–16). The apostle Paul writes that the promised seed refers in particular to Christ (Gal. 3:16).

The Abrahamic covenant is described as such:

1. Exclusive. It is only for Abraham and his (spiritual) descendants (Gen. 17:7).

2. Everlasting. It is not replaced by any later covenant (Gen. 17:7).

3. Accepted by faith, not works. "Abram believed the LORD, and it was credited to him as righteousness" (Gen. 15:6).

4. The external sign of entering into the Abrahamic covenant was circumcision (Gen. 17:10), but it has to be matched by an internal change, the circumcision of the heart (Jer. 4:4).

5. According to Paul, since the Abrahamic covenant is eternal, the followers of Christ are "children of Abraham" and therefore part of this covenant through faith. "Understand, then, that those who have faith are children of Abraham" (Gal. 3:7).

6. According to covenant theology, Paul makes it clear that baptism is the external sign of faith in Christ ("You were baptized into Christ"), and that through faith in Christ the believer is part of the Abrahamic covenant ("Abraham's seed"). This provides the basis for the doctrine that baptism is the New Testament sign of God's covenant with Abraham (Gal. 3:26). Noncovenantal theology does not believe that the Abrahamic covenant is inherited by Gentiles and thus has a different view of baptism.

7. Romans 11 teaches disobedient Jews are broken off the family tree of Abraham. It is only after the full number of the Gentiles has been grafted into Abraham's family tree that God will pour out His mercy on the people of Israel.

The Promise of God to Abram

The Abrahamic Covenant was made by God with Abram in Genesis 12:1–3. "The LORD had said to Abram, 'Leave your country, your people and your father's household and go to the land I will show you. I will make you into a great nation and I will bless you; I will make your name great, and you will be a blessing. I will bless those who bless you, and whoever curses you I will curse; and all peoples on earth will be blessed through you.'"

The Lord instructed Abram (later God changed his name to Abraham) to take his family from their home in Ur and go to a new land called Canaan. This was an unconditional covenant that contained four primary provisions:

- I will make you into a great nation, and I will bless you.
- I will make your name great, and you will be a blessing.
- I will bless those who bless you, and whoever curses you, I will curse.
- All peoples on earth will be blessed through you.

God was indeed giving a special favor to Abraham and his descendants. God's promises are never broken, and this was no exception, as the pledge is renewed several times in Scripture to Abraham's descendants through Isaac and Jacob.

The Promised Land

The promised land of the Abrahamic covenant given Abraham is first described in Genesis 13:15–17: "All the land that you see I will give to you and your offspring forever. I will make your offspring like the dust of the earth, so that if anyone could count the dust, then your offspring could be counted. Go, walk through the length and breadth of the land, for I am giving it to you."

The boundaries were not clearly defined at this first mention, but they certainly are in the next reference to the land: "On that day the LORD made a covenant with Abram and said, 'To your descendants I give this land, from the river of Egypt to the great river, the Euphrates—the land of the Kenites, Kenizzites, Kadmonites, Hittites, Perizzites, Rephaites, Amorites, Canaanites, Girgashites and Jebusites'" (Gen. 15:18–21).

Later, under the rule of King David, we can see that the nation of Israel indeed encompassed all the land between the Nile River (Egypt) and the Euphrates River (through present-day Iraq). Verification of the land under David's reign can be found in 2 Samuel 8:3, Deuteronomy 1:7, and Deuteronomy 11:24.

In Joshua 1:4, God confirms the boundaries as the Israelites were about to cross the Jordan River into their land. "Your territory will extend from the desert to Lebanon, and from the great river, the Euphrates—all the Hittite country—to the Great Sea on the west" (the Mediterranean Sea). King Solomon retained control over these borders, as seen in 1 Kings 4:21, 24. As God said, the land is His and is to be inhabited by His people for all generations of Abraham, Isaac, and Jacob. However, it has consistently been a struggle for Abraham's descendants to keep that land.

From the biblical patriarchs up to the twentieth century, the land fell under a number of ruling empires due in part to the Hebrews' disobedience to the covenants of God. Some of those conquering empires include

- the Babylonian, under Nebuchadnezzar;
- the Greek, under Alexander the Great;
- the Turkish Ottoman Empire, under Sultan Suleiman; and
- the Roman Empire, under Constantine.

And in the twentieth century, the British ruled the land until the rebirth of Israel as a sovereign nation in 1948. There have been many attempts to keep the Jewish people out of their promised land, but they have intermittently, albeit temporarily, returned to it. They have suffered through battles, massacres, the Holocaust, and have been scattered throughout the world. Yet God promised they would return to the land that is theirs, and they have increasingly been streaming in since the 1948 rebirth.

Everlasting Promises

The Abrahamic covenant was confirmed with a covenant ceremony of circumcision in Genesis 17:10–14. This was required as a token or sign of their commitment to God. The provisions of this agreement are permanent. "I will establish my covenant as an everlasting covenant between me and you and your descendants after you for the generations to come, to be your God and the God of your descendants after you. The whole land of Canaan, where you are now an alien, I will give as an everlasting possession to you and your descendants after you; and I will be their God" (Gen. 17:7–8).

This is God's pledge to be the Abba Father of His people and the one who provides for them with guarantees for their future blessings. Through numerous scientific, medical, and technical inventions and wonders, the great influence of the Jewish people on the world is undeniable. They have won Nobel prizes in physics, economics, and the arts. God has surely blessed the nations through His people, as Genesis 12 states.

Though the Jewish people have violated doing their part in the covenants with God, He promises that they will someday repent and return to Him as their God (Zech. 12:10–14). Romans 11:26–27 says, "As it is written: The deliverer will come from Zion; he will turn godlessness away from Jacob [Israel], And this is my covenant with them when I take away their sins."

The Abrahamic covenant will be ultimately fulfilled with the return of the Messiah. The final blessings bestowed on His people will be reconciliation with God as their God in His kingdom reign on earth.

Mosaic Covenant

The Mosaic covenant is found in Exodus 19 and 24.

The book of Deuteronomy expands on the Abrahamic promise of a people and a land. Repeatedly mentioned is the promise of the Lord, "I will be your God and you will be My people." God particularly displayed as his glory-presence comes to dwell in the midst of the people. This covenant is the one most in view by the term *old covenant*.

The Content

The Mosaic covenant was made between God and the nation of Israel and can be found in Exodus 19 and 24 and Deuteronomy 5:6–22. This covenant is often referred to as the law. Others call it the Sinaic covenant since it took place at Mt. Sinai.

A large part of the Mosaic covenant was the Ten Commandments (the reason for it being called the law), and with them God promised

- to make the Hebrew people His special people among all nations if they keep God's Commandments,
- to make the people of Israel a holy nation and a kingdom of priest, and
- to give them the Sabbath for a day of rest and told them it is to be kept holy.

The Law Exposes Sin

Under the Mosaic covenant, the promise of righteousness in daily life could only be acquired by fulfilling the works of the law. But since we are prisoners of sin, only in the Messiah could the covenant promise be fulfilled (Deut. 6:25, Gal. 3:21).

When looking at the covenant, we see that it can be separated into these categories:

- Spiritual commands (Exod. 20:2–8; Deut. 5:6–12)
- Moral and social conduct (Exod. 20:12–17; Deut. 5:16–21)
- Ceremonial (regarding the tabernacle; Exod. 25–27; Exod. 30)
- Requirements for priestly garments (Exod. 28–29)

The commandments God gave the Israelites were, without doubt, violated. In fact, they cannot be kept by any human, as we all are imperfect.

- Everyone has sinned (Rom. 3:23).
- The penalty for our sin is death (Rom. 6:23).
- Jesus Christ died as payment for our sins (Rom. 5:8).
- To be forgiven for our sin, we must believe and confess that Jesus is Lord and acknowledge that salvation comes through Jesus Christ (Rom. 10:8–10).

Romans 3:20 says, "Therefore no one will be declared righteous in His sight by observing the law; rather, through the law we become conscious of sin." Without the law, we cannot be aware of what God declares iniquities. The law was given as guidelines to live by and shows us where we go wrong. It is a template by which to pattern our lives.

Mosaic Covenant: Fulfillment

By failing to keep the Mosaic covenant, the Israelites paved the way for God's new covenant, which would bring about the only way for them (and us) to have reconciliation with God.

> *But now a righteousness from God, apart from law, has been made known, to which the Law and the Prophets testify. (Ezek. 36:24–29 KJV)*

> *This righteousness from God comes through faith in Jesus Christ to all who believe. There is no difference, for all have sinned*

*and fall short of the glory of God, and are
justified freely by his grace through the
redemption that came by Christ Jesus.
(Rom. 3:21–24 KJV)*

Galatians 3:24–25 (KJV) puts it this way: "So the law
was put in charge to lead us to Christ that we might be justified by faith. Now that faith has come, we are no longer
under the supervision of the law."

Davidic Covenant

The Davidic covenant is found in 2 Samuel 7.

The Lord proclaims that He will build a house and lin-
eage for David, establishing His kingdom and throne forever.
This covenant is appealed to as God preserves David's descendants despite their wickedness (cf. 1 Kings 11:26–39, 15:1–
8; 2 Kings 8:19, 19:32–34), although it did not stop judgment from finally arriving (compare 2 Kings 21:7, 23:26–27
and Jeremiah 13:12–14). Among the prophets of the exile,
there is hope of restoration under a Davidic king who will
bring peace and justice (Ezek. 37:24–28).

The New Covenant

The new covenant is anticipated with the hopes of the
Davidic messiah, and most explicitly predicted by the prophet
Jeremiah (Jer. 31:34). At the Last Supper, Jesus alludes to this
prophecy, as well as to prophecies, such as Isaiah 49:8, when
he says that the cup of the Passover meal is "the New Covenant
in [his] blood." This use of the Old Testament typology is

developed further in the Epistle to the Hebrews (see especially chapters 7–10). Jesus is the last Adam and Israel's hope and consolation; He is the fulfillment of the law and the prophets (Matt. 5:17–18). He is the prophet greater than Jonah (Matt. 12:41) and the Son over the house where Moses was a servant (Heb. 3:5–6), leading his people to the heavenly promised land. He is the high priest greater than Aaron, offering up himself as the perfect sacrifice once and for all (Heb. 9:12, 26). He is the king greater than Solomon (Matt. 12:42), ruling forever on David's throne (Luke 1:32). The term New Testament comes from the Latin translation of the Greek *new covenant* and is most often used for the collection of books in the Bible, can also refer to the new covenant as a theological concept.

Everything in the Bible was written for us, but not necessarily to us. The New Testament is made up of twenty-seven books, of which nine are written primarily to the Jews, nine were written primarily to the Gentile church, and nine were written to a mixture to both Jew and Gentile. Peter, James, Jude, and John wrote the following books to teach the Jews correct interpretation of their doctrine, to correct their conduct, and to bridge them over to a better covenant by accepting Jesus as their messiah. They wrote Hebrews, James, 1 Peter, 2 Peter, 1 John, 2 John, 3 John, Jude, and Revelation, primarily to the Jews.

Paul, on the other hand, was sent to the Gentiles and wrote Romans, showing the doctrine of God's grace; 1 Corinthians and 2 Corinthians to show God's love with some reproofs; Galatians to correct doctrine; Ephesians for the doctrines of marriage, wealth, walk, warfare, and order; Philippians and Colossians for correction; 1 Thessalonians and 2 Thessalonians to give the church hope in the last days, and introduced the doctrine of the catching away of the church.

> *All scripture is given by inspiration of God, and is profitable for doctrine, for reproof, for correction, for instruction in righteousness. (2 Tim. 3:16 KJV)*

The church did not replace the Jews or old covenant, but God added a new better covenant and the two contracts still live side by side today. Someday the Jews will accept Jesus as their Savior.

The stories in the Bible are mostly about Jesus and redemption and often have deeper meanings. The Passover story where God revealed His power to the world by releasing Israel from Egyptian bondage is rich in spiritual truths and symbology of things to come. His plan for world deliverance, sanctification, Holy Spirit, authority over evil, rewards, and eternal life in heaven is all outlined through Bible stories. In the Passover story, the steps of salvation are clear. Take a lamb for each person or family, keep it a while and get attached to it, then kill it, eat all of it, put the blood on the doorposts, and the death angel will pass by your household. Next, get your traveling clothes on and be ready to leave in the morning. The steps for mankind's salvation follow a similar pattern. We learn about Jesus, accept Him as our Savior, and accept the work He did on the cross. We spiritually receive His shed blood on our hearts for forgiveness of sins and for eternal life in heaven. Next, we wander through life full of hardships, sacrifices, making mistakes but learning how to partner with God. Overcoming the problems of life and entering into the promised land. We start to make fewer mistakes and learn to submit, obey, and counsel with God. We cross over the Jordan River and take the promised land with power, knowing who we are in Christ. God saved the Hebrews in the Old Testament on credit because Jesus had not gone to the cross yet. But for us Gentiles, looking back at the cross, salvation is all paid for.

God's Plan Is Salvation for the Gentiles (The Book of Ruth)

The names of all the characters have meaning in the story of Ruth, who was a Gentile. The story starts with a famine (no bread) in Bethlehem (which means "house of bread"). This famine caused Elimelech (which means "God is King") to take his wife, Naomi (happy), and two children, Mahlon (sick) and Chilion (weak), to Moab, a Gentile nation. Mahlon marries Ruth (companion, beautiful), and Chilion marries Orpah (stiff-necked, stubborn). Jesus (the bread of life) will be born in the future in this "house of bread" (Bethlehem) in a manger, where sheep are fed (metaphorically speaking, we are sheep). Bread is a staple of life; Jesus gives eternal life.

Ten years later, Naomi returns to Bethlehem having lost her husband, both kids, and land in Israel and wants to be called Marah (sorrow). She tries to separate herself from Ruth and Orpah. Orpah leaves and goes back to Moab to join Israel's enemies. But Ruth insists on following her back to Israel, accepts her God, and takes care of the aging Naomi.

Prophetically speaking, Naomi is a type of Israel who returns to their land (1948), after the Holocaust of WWII. Ruth is a metaphor for Gentile Christian, a New Testament church that supports Israel and takes care of her and worships her God. Orpah is a symbol of Islam that leaves Israel and joins the Gentile nations.

Ruth (the gentile church) works in the harvest fields, winning souls, represented by the grain. Boaz (kinsman redeemer) sees her and helps her get grain (souls). Barley harvest starts in May–June, at the same time Gentile Christianity started at Pentecost. Boaz gives six measures of barley to Ruth, symbolizing the six days of her work (six millennia), then she enters the seventh day of rest and they are betrothed, which may be a metaphor of the last millennium, where Christ reigns on earth. Ruth is refused marriage by a close unnamed relative (maybe Satan, who has authority over all sinners); Boaz is a type of Christ the Redeemer who took a Gentile bride, Ruth, a type of Christianity, and restores the land to Naomi (Israel) in the seventh day of rest. The wedding day of the Lord is at the end of this age at Jesus's second coming.

The Book of Ester

The story of Ester parallels the book of Revelation, where God's chosen are saved and Satan is thrown into the lake of fire. Ester is a shadow of Christianity and Hamon and his ten sons, a type of antichrist, and the ten kings are a symbol of the ten nations discussed in Daniel 2:42–44 (ten toes), Daniel 7:24 (ten horns are kings), and Revelation 17:12 (ten nations).

The life of Joseph is another example of God's plan. It parallels the life of Christ.

God's Plans Revealed in the Life of Joseph (Genesis 37–50)

Even though Jesus and Joseph lived more than 1,700 years apart, they both had parallel lives. Again, God shows a pattern of His future plans about a coming Savior. Both were shepherds, both were sent out by their fathers to their brethren, both were rejected, both had a special coat given to them by their father, both coats were dipped in blood, both became servants, both were taken to Egypt, both resisted temptations, both had visions of the future, both were falsely accused, both tested people to reveal their true motives, both were promoted to a new life, both forgave their accusers, both were not recognized by their brothers, and both became royalty. Just to mention a few parallel aspects of the life of Jesus and Joseph. The life of Joseph takes up thirteen chapters in Genesis, so it must be important.

God's Salvation Plans Symbolized in the Tabernacle Design

God gave Moses the Ten Commandments on Mt. Sinai, and at the same time, God showed Moses a physical representation of the spiritual path for mankind to follow to reach God. He showed Moses the tabernacle (Exod. 25–27) and told him to build it according to the heavenly pattern.

The tabernacle had a wide gate on the east side to allow anyone access who wanted to seek God and become free of the bondage of sin. It was a rectangular shape that was twice as deep (east to west) as it was wide (north to south). God was on the far west side of the tabernacle, hidden from view, housed in a cubical-shaped structure with no windows. From man's point of view, entering the wide gate, he could not see God but first encountered a square sacrificial altar from unfinished stone. This altar represented the first part of God's plan for the salvation of mankind through the shed blood of an innocent animal and later represented the cross, where God Himself would pay the price once and for all mankind through the blood sacrifice of His Son, Jesus Christ. The next item a man would encounter traveling west toward God was the laver. It was a circular bath of water for ceremonial cleansing made from copper looking glasses that had been taken from Egypt during the exodus. It may represent looking at one's own reflection spiritually and desiring to be made clean in God's sight. Later, for the church, it represented baptism, another step of obedience toward God. Continuing west toward God, we go up five stairs to a new level, where we will learn about God the Holy Spirit, fellowship, and worship. We enter a room that has no light except for a candlestick on the left (south) side, with seven lamps and all made of solid gold. Gold represents the deity of God, and since the candlestick is solid gold, it represents God and the lamps, His enlightening power of the Holy Spirit. Across the room from the candlestick on our right (north side) is a table with two loaves of bread, representing the two covenants (law and grace). Bread represents fellowship and may represent communion for the church. Jesus said he was the bread of life. Continuing west toward God, we encounter a smoking pot of incense that represents our worship and praises toward God, and at the back of the room, a large thick curtain separating the Hebrew from the presence of God, but for the church it is torn in half from top to bottom by the work of Jesus Christ on the cross, allowing access to God. On the other side of the curtain is the ark of the covenant, made of wood overlaid with gold, and above the lid of the ark dwells the presence of God. The lid is called the mercy seat, and the wood overlaid with gold represents both the humanity of Christ, and the gold His deity.

From God's perspective looking east, He first sees worship and then fellowship through the Holy Spirit (the incense, candlestick, and bread on the table). So if you want to know God in a deeper way, learn to spend more time with Him, be born again by asking for the Holy Spirit, and learn to worship God.

We Are a Tabernacle

The tabernacle may also symbolize the three parts of mankind. The outer court representing our body, where we accept Jesus and are baptized into Christ; the inner court, where our souls are enlightened and we worship and have communion with one another; and the holy of holies representing our spirit man that communicates directly with God. After Christ died on the cross and rose from the dead, the holy of holies and inner court became one when the curtain separating the two was torn from top to bottom.

The tabernacle may also symbolize each believer who no longer stands on the earth but is seated in heavenly places. The tabernacle foundation stands on silver sockets (a form of righteousness) and didn't touch the earth (which was cursed by sin), and the linen covering with cherubim on the roof provides protection.

The USA Is Patterned after the Tabernacle

Surprisingly, the United States matches the pattern of the tabernacle. People seeking freedom from Spain, England, and Ireland came into Ellis Island at the east gate of the nation. Spain was expelling Jews who fled to America looking for a new home. The gate was wide, accepting everyone. "Give me your tired, your poor, etc." First, there was war with the French and Indians, then with England, and finally the Civil War, spilling much blood on US East Coast. This may represent the altar and blood sacrifice on the east end of the tabernacle. Then traveling west, the Great Lakes, the Mississippi River, and its tributaries were reached, which provided expansion and may represent the laver bath. They provided new avenues to the west. The Great Plains was at a higher elevation, like the five steps going up from the outer court to the holy place. In Texas and Oklahoma to the south, oil was discovered and may represent the oil lampstand on the left in the holy place. To the north was the breadbasket of the nation in the form of wheat fields, just like the holy place north side, which has the table with loaves of bread. Yellowstone may represent the seething pot of incense, representing worship, and the Rocky Mountains the curtain separating the holy place from the holy of holies. Gold was discovered in 1849 in the San Joaquin Valley, California, representing the golden ark. Provision of fruits, vegetables, wine, and plenty has poured from this California location, feeding the entire nation throughout the history of America. The recent drought and fires in California may be a wake-up call from God for us to recognize who is really providing for this nation. Have we forgotten to give thanks to our source and become prideful and self-sufficient in our own eyes?

God's Plan as Seen Through the Bible Festivals

God also gave the Hebrews seven festivals or feasts to celebrate each year (three in the spring, one in the summer, and three in the fall). They were to follow certain rituals during these feast days that are rich in symbolism, showing God's plans in the future.

The spring festivals are Passover, Unleavened Bread, and First Fruits, and the summer festival of Pentecost were fulfilled in Christ's first coming. Passover represents Jesus dying on the cross for the sins of the world and resurrecting back to life the third day. The Hebrews experienced a shadow of this truth when they were delivered from Egyptian bondage. The blood of the lamb saved them from the death angel. In like manner, the true lamb of God shed His blood to cover the sins of mankind, and those who believe this have salvation. Referenced in (Romans 4:25), it says we are *justified* by the work Jesus did for us on the cross. The feast of Unleavened Bread speaks to the sinless nature of Jesus. Leaven (yeast) is a symbol of sin. Next is the festival of First Fruits, which again points to Jesus as the first man to rise from the dead and getting a new body equipped for eternal life in heaven. Pentecost, or Festival of Weeks, celebrates the pouring out of Holy Spirit into mankind. The process of sanctification (1 Thess. 4:3) is next after we receive the Holy Spirit, which is the road to holiness. This festival was fulfilled in Acts 2:38 and continues today.

The fall festivals Rosh Hashanah (Trumpets), Yom Kippur (Atonement), and Sukkot (Kingdom Living) have not been fulfilled yet. Based on the rituals of each festival given by Moses in the Old Testament, Trumpets may represent the catching away of the church, like Enoch was caught up to heaven; Atonement may be the tribulation period where people have a last chance to be saved; and Kingdom may represent God taking back the earth and/or dwelling with us (tabernacling with us) during the millennial kingdom age. The festivals all show the grace of God touching our reality in some way.

Numbers in Design

Our universe has been designed and contains many symbiotic relationships between plants, animals, and minerals. Even magnetism, momentum, gravity, speed, and electronics follow simple mathematical rules. Like God Himself, His creation is perfect, and Numbers in the Bible show the design of Creation. Mathematics is used to explore these relationships and the laws that govern them. We have simple formulas that can reveal important information about the world around us. For example, What is the area of my rectangular living room or a circle? Or how much fuel can I put into my cylindrical fuel tank? Even our clothing can be reduced down to numerical sizes: I wear size 11 shoe, size 44 long shirts, and my hat size is an 8. Numbers are a perfect science and reflect God's perfection. The Bible often shows God's design of creation and His plans for planet Earth.

Jesus, in describing the kingdom of God in Matthew 13:47–49, says that it is like casting a fishing net that catches fish, and again in John 21:6, Jesus demonstrates this principle using a miracle that contains more exact information. Jesus introduces the number 153, the number of fish in the net. This number has surprising characteristics that only now is being fully understood. At the beginning of His ministry, Jesus told His disciples to follow Him and He would make them fishers of men, and at the end of His ministry, recorded in John 21:6, the disciples caught exactly 153 fish, and none escaped the net! This number is the sum of all the numbers between 1 and 17 (1 + 2 + 3 + 4 +...17 = 153). It is a triangular number in that it can be arranged in a triangle, corresponding to the Trinity. When each integer of 153 is multiplied by itself three times and added together, the sum comes back to itself, 153 (1 x 1 x 1 + 5 x 5 x 5 + 3 x 3 x 3 = 153)! It is the only number that does this. For this reason, it is called the resurrection number. It resurrects itself, just like Jesus. Not only that, but any number divisible by three can be reduced to 153 by repeating this same function several times. This may imply that one-third of mankind will be resurrected and go to heaven (*Prophecy in the News*, February 2015, p. 12).

Gods' Plan for a Savior

> *God so loved the world that He gave His*
> *only begotten son that whosoever believed in*
> *Him should not perish, but have everlasting*
> *life. (John 3:16 KJV)*

Attributes of the Blood of Christ

The blood of Jesus was without the original sin that was passed down from Adam through the male DNA. The male always determines a baby's blood type. The mother's placenta keeps the baby's blood from mingling with the mother's blood. This is why the virgin birth was necessary. The blood of Jesus is holy and very precious. It came from the Father through the virgin birth (Heb. 10:29; Acts 20:28).

> *Of how much sorer punishment, suppose ye,*
> *shall he be thought worthy, who hath trod-*
> *den underfoot the Son of God, and hath*
> *counted the blood of the covenant, where-*
> *with he was sanctified, an unholy thing,*
> *and hath done despite unto the Spirit of*
> *grace? (Heb. 10:29 KJV)*

> *Take heed therefore unto yourselves, and to*
> *all the flock, over the which the Holy Ghost*
> *hath made you overseers, to feed the church*
> *of God, which he hath purchased with his*
> *own blood. (Acts 20:28 KJV)*

The blood can somehow speak to God (Gen. 4:10).

> *And he said, what hast thou done? the voice of thy brother's blood crieth unto me from the ground [Abel's blood cries for vengeance here]. (Gen 4:10 KJV)*

But the blood of Jesus speaks to God for mercy in Hebrews 12:24.

> *And to Jesus the mediator of the new covenant, and to the blood of sprinkling, that speaketh better things than that of Abel [vengeance versus mercy]. (Heb. 12:24 KJV)*

It is incorruptible, everlasting (1 Pet. 1:18–19).

> *Forasmuch as ye know that ye were not redeemed with corruptible things, as silver and gold, from your vain conversation received by tradition from your fathers; But with the precious blood of Christ, as of a lamb without blemish and without spot. (1 Pet. 1:18–19 KJV)*

The blood of Jesus was innocent blood, not subject to penalty (Matt. 27:4).

> *Saying, I have sinned in that I have betrayed the innocent blood. (Matt. 27:4 KJV)*

It gives access to God's throne (Heb. 10:19).

> *Having therefore, brethren, boldness to enter into the holiest by the blood of Jesus, By a new and living way, which he hath consecrated for us, through the veil, that is to say, his flesh. (Heb 10:19–20 KJV)*

It redeems slaves of sin (Heb. 9:12; Rev. 5:9).

> *Neither by the blood of goats and calves, but by his own blood he entered in once into the holy place, having obtained eternal redemption for us. (Heb. 9:12 KJV)*

It purchased the church (Acts 20:28).

> *Take heed therefore unto yourselves, and to all the flock, over the which the Holy Ghost hath made you overseers, to feed the church of God, which he hath purchased with his own blood. (Acts 20:28 KJV)*

It saves from the pit (Zech. 9:11).

> *As for thee also, by the blood of thy covenant I have sent forth thy prisoners out of the pit wherein is no water. (Zech. 9:11 KJV)*

It makes peace between races, social status, levels, and genders (Gal. 3:28; Col. 3:11).

> *There is neither Jew nor Greek, there is neither bond nor free, there is neither male nor female: for ye are all one in Christ Jesus. (Gal 3:28 KJV)*

> *Where there is neither Greek nor Jew, circumcision nor uncircumcision, Barbarian, Scythian, bond nor free: but Christ is all, and in all. (Col. 3:11 KJV)*

It protects from the destroyer (Exod. 12:23).

> *For the LORD will pass through to smite the Egyptians; and when he seeth the blood upon the lintel, and on the two side posts, the LORD will pass over the door, and will not suffer the destroyer to come in unto your houses to smite you. (Exod. 12:23 KJV)*

It atones or covers the soul (Lev. 17:11).

> *For the life of the flesh is in the blood: and I have given it to you upon the altar to make an atonement for your souls: for it is the blood that maketh an atonement for the soul. (Lev. 17:11 KJV)*

It perfects us (Heb. 10:14, 13:20–21).

> *For by one offering he hath perfected forever*
> *them that are sanctified. (Heb. 10:14 KJV)*

> *Now the God of peace, that brought again*
> *from the dead our Lord Jesus, that great*
> *shepherd of the sheep, through the blood of*
> *the everlasting covenant, [21] Make you*
> *perfect in every good work to do his will,*
> *working in you that which is well pleasing*
> *in his sight, through Jesus Christ; to whom*
> *be glory for ever and ever. Amen. (Heb.*
> *13:20 KJV)*

It sanctifies men (Heb. 13:12).

> *Wherefore Jesus also, that he might sanctify*
> *the people with his own blood, suffered*
> *without the gate. (Heb. 13:12 KJV)*

It heals sickness (1 Pet. 2:24).

> *Who his own self bare our sins in his own*
> *body on the tree, that we, being dead to sins,*
> *should live unto righteousness: by whose*
> *stripes ye were healed. (1 Pet. 2:24 KJV)*

The ceremonial cleansing is a shadow of Christ's work
on the cross.

> *The LORD said to Moses, These are the reg-*
> *ulations for the diseased person at the time*

of his ceremonial cleansing, when he is brought to the priest: The priest is to go outside the camp and examine him. If the person has been healed of his infectious skin disease, the priest shall order that two live clean birds and some cedar wood, scarlet yarn and hyssop be brought for the one to be cleansed. Then the priest shall order that one of the birds be killed over fresh water in a clay pot. He is then to take the live bird and dip it, together with the cedar wood, the scarlet yarn and the hyssop, into the blood of the bird that was killed over the fresh water. Seven times he shall sprinkle the one to be cleansed of the infectious disease and pronounce him clean. Then he is to release the live bird in the open fields. (Lev. 14:1–7 KJV)

Symbols of the Cleansing Ceremony

- Skin disease or leprosy is a symbol of sin.
- Jesus died on the cross outside the camp (Jerusalem).
- Two birds may represent Jesus's two natures: (1) Son of Man and (2) Son of God.
- The first bird represents Jesus's body, which died on the cross, the second bird his resurrected body, which went to the Father.
- Cedarwood is a symbol of the cross.

- Scarlet yarn is a symbol of the shed blood and suffering of Christ.
- By hyssop the blood was applied; by faith we apply the blood today.
- Jesus shed His blood seven times:
  1. Jesus sweat drops of blood from His skin in Gethsemane.
  2. From His back when whipped.
  3. From His face when His beard was pulled out.
  4. From His forehead from the crown of thorns.
  5. From His hands on the cross.
  6. From His feet on the cross.
  7. From His side on the cross.
- The clay pot may represent Christ's earthly body, and the fresh water His righteousness.

The priest is to take some of the blood of the guilt offering and put it on the lobe of the right ear of the one to be cleansed, on the thumb of his right hand and on the big toe of his right foot. The priest shall then take some of the log of oil, pour it in the palm of his own left hand, dip his right forefinger into the oil in his palm, and with his finger sprinkle some of it before the LORD seven times. The priest is to put some of the oil remaining in his palm on the lobe of the right ear of the one to be cleansed, on the thumb of his right hand and on the big toe of his right foot, on top of the blood of the

> *guilt offering. The rest of the oil in his palm*
> *the priest shall put on the head of the one to*
> *be cleansed and make atonement for him*
> *before the LORD. (Lev. 14:14–18 KJV)*

The right ear symbolizes our hearing or mind. With our minds and personality, we relate to other people. The right big toe may symbolize a person's walk. We relate to God with our spirit.

The right thumb symbolizes a person's work. With our body we relate to the physical world. You cannot pound a nail into a board with your spirit or soul.

> *But if we walk in the light, as he is in the*
> *light, we have fellowship one with another,*
> *and the blood of Jesus Christ his Son*
> *cleanseth us from all sin. (1 John 1:7 KJV)*

> *What the blood covers is anointed with the*
> *Holy Spirit (oil). (Lev. 8:22–32 KJV)*

It gives us victory (Col. 2:15).

> *And having spoiled principalities and pow-*
> *ers, he made a show of them openly, tri-*
> *umphing over them in it. (Col. 2:15 KJV)*

It blots out Old Testament ordinances (Col. 2:14).

> *Blotting out the handwriting of ordinances*
> *that was against us, which was contrary to*
> *us, and took it out of the way, nailing it to*
> *his cross. (Col. 2:14 KJV)*

It washes and whitens us (Rev. 1:5; Ps. 51:7).

> *And from Jesus Christ, who is the faithful witness, and the first begotten of the dead, and the prince of the kings of the earth. Unto him that loved us, and washed us from our sins in his own blood. (Rev. 1:5 KJV)*

> *Purge me with hyssop, and I shall be clean: wash me, and I shall be whiter than snow. (Ps. 51:7 KJV)*

It cleanses us continually from sin (1 John 1:7; Rev. 7:14).

> *But if we walk in the light, as he is in the light, we have fellowship one with another, and the blood of Jesus Christ his Son cleanseth us from all sin. (1 John 1:7 KJV)*

> *And I said unto him, Sir, thou knowest. And he said to me, These are they which came out of great tribulation, and have washed their robes, and made them white in the blood of the Lamb. (Rev. 7:14 KJV)*

It purges the conscience (Heb. 9:14).

> *How much more shall the blood of Christ, who through the eternal Spirit offered himself without spot to God, purge your conscience from dead works to serve the living God? (Heb. 9:14 KJV)*

It cancels sin (Heb. 9:22).

And almost all things are by the law purged with blood; and without shedding of blood is no remission. (Heb. 9:22 KJV)

It provides forgiveness of sin (Eph. 1:7).

In whom we have redemption through his blood, the forgiveness of sins, according to the riches of his grace. (Eph. 1:7 KJV)

It justifies sinners by faith (Rom. 5:9).

Much more then, being now justified by his blood, we shall be saved from wrath through him. (Rom. 5:9 KJV)

The accuser is overcome *because* of the blood (Rev. 12:11).

And they overcame him by the blood of the Lamb, and by the word of their testimony; and they loved not their lives unto the death. (Rev. 12:11 KJV)

It establishes fellowship of believers (1 Cor. 10:16).

The cup of blessing which we bless, is it not the communion of the blood of Christ? The bread which we break, is it not the communion of the body of Christ? For we being many are one bread, and one body: for we are all partakers of that one bread. (1 Cor. 10:16–17 KJV)

It ratifies our covenant with God (Exod. 25:4–8, Heb. 9:18–20).

> *Whereupon neither the first testament was dedicated without blood. For when Moses had spoken every precept to all the people according to the law, he took the blood of calves and of goats, with water, and scarlet wool, and hyssop, and sprinkled both the book, and all the people, Saying, This is the blood of the testament which God hath enjoined unto you. (Heb. 9:18–20 KJV)*

As the blood of Jesus covered His body on the cross, so does His blood cover His earthly body (the church) now. It is life and dispels sin and death as light dispels darkness. It is because of the blood that we are in the kingdom of God and have authority in Christ to wear His armor and operate against all darkness.

Jesus was born in Bethlehem, meaning "house of bread." He was born in a manger, where sheep feed themselves. He is our bread of life. We are "His sheep," and His shed blood is the new contract between man and God for salvation.

God's plan is to give mankind His Holy Spirit.

Symbolized by oil.

This process is symbolized in the Old Testament as being similar to applying oil to the skin that soaks in providing health and cleansing.

The word *Christ* comes from the Greek word *Christos*, meaning "anointed." *Christos* comes from the root word

Chrio, meaning "to smear or rub with oil." *Messiah* means anointed one and comes from the Hebrew word *mashiyach*. Mashiyach comes from the root word *mashach*, meaning to rub with oil or anoint. So in both the Hebrew and Greek, Christ the Messiah means the same: to be anointed and rubbed with oil.

When oil is applied to the body, it soaks in and becomes part of us. Like the oil, Holy Spirit becomes part of us when invited.

The word *anointing* is first used in Exodus 30:22–25 and describes the characteristics of the holy anointing oil through the four principal spices and the amount of each one.

> *Moreover the* LORD *spoke unto Moses, saying, Take thou also unto thee principal spices, of pure myrrh five hundred [shekels], and of sweet cinnamon half so much, [even] two hundred and fifty [shekels], and of sweet calamus two hundred and fifty [shekels], And of cassia five hundred [shekels], after the shekel of the sanctuary, and of oil olive an hin: and thou shalt make it an oil of holy ointment, an ointment compound after the art of the apothecary: it shall be an holy anointing oil. (Exod. 30:22–25 KJV)*

A hin of oil is about five quarts. The myrrh and cassia were the main ingredients of five hundred shekels each (about a cup). Myrrh was a costly Arabic gum from the bark of a tree used to relieve pain. Cassia was a laxative used to purge and cleanse the body. They represent the main work of the Holy Spirit to heal, relieve pain, and clean (deliver us from evil).

Cinnamon may represent the zeal or fire of God. Jesus displayed this attribute when He turned over the money changers tables in the temple. Calamus was an aromatic perfume from an Egyptian water plant or reed. It had a bulbous round base with the fragrant sap inside. It may represent the gentleness of the Holy Spirit.

> *A bruised reed shall he not break, and the smoking flax shall he not quench: he shall bring forth judgment unto truth. (Isa. 42:3 KJV)*

The Holy Spirit Has These Attributes

God enabled (anointed) people in the Old Testament to perform certain offices. Some were anointed prophets, some priests, and some kings. God also anointed people for certain tasks. Samson was anointed for strength, Joshua for a conquering warrior, and Solomon for wisdom to lead his people. Oil was used often to signify or symbolize the anointing. Oil has properties that parallel the enabling power of God the Holy Spirit. When applied to the body, it soaks in and becomes part of the body. It makes the skin look healthy and shiny. When the glory of God soaked into Moses on the mount, it caused his face to shine.

> *And, behold, I send the promise of my Father upon you: but tarry ye in the city of Jerusalem, until ye be endued with power from on high. (Luke 24:49 KJV)*

He that believeth and is baptized shall be saved; but he that believeth not shall be damned. And these signs shall follow them that believe; In my name shall they cast out devils; they shall speak with new tongues; They shall take up serpents; and if they drink any deadly thing, it shall not hurt them; they shall lay hands on the sick, and they shall recover. (Mark 16:16–18 KJV)

But ye shall receive power, after that the Holy Ghost is come upon you: and ye shall be witnesses unto me both in Jerusalem, and in all Judaea, and in Samaria, and unto the uttermost part of the earth. (Acts 1:8 KJV)

We can see the anointing in action through Jesus. Jesus was anointed with the Holy Spirit and power (Acts 10:38 KJV) above that of His brethren. Jesus said, "The Spirit of the Lord [is] upon me, because he hath anointed me to preach the gospel to the poor; he hath sent me to heal the broken-hearted, to preach deliverance to the captives, and recovering of sight to the blind, to set at liberty them that are bruised" (Luke 4:18 KJV). Jesus was anointed an apostle (Heb. 3:1), He was anointed a prophet (Luke 4:24), He was anointed a shepherd (pastor) (John 10:14; 1 Pet. 5:4), and He was anointed a teacher (Matt. 9:35). Jesus was anointed without measure (John 3:34). This implies that the Holy Spirit is given to us by measure. When Saul, who was anointed king, tried to function as a priest, God became angry. He was not anointed priest. Maybe this points to the fact we should be aware of the gifts God has distributed to each one of us and not covet, get jealous, or operate outside of our calling.

> *How God anointed Jesus of Nazareth with the Holy Ghost and with power: who went about doing good, and healing all that were oppressed of the devil; for God was with him. (Acts 10:38 KJV)*

> *But the anointing which ye have received of him abideth in you, and ye need not that any man teach you: but as the same anointing teacheth you of all things, and is truth, and is no lie, and even as it hath taught you, ye shall abide in him. (1 Job 2:27 KJV)*

> *And it shall come to pass in that day, that his burden shall be taken away from off thy shoulder, and his yoke from off thy neck, and the yoke shall be destroyed because of the anointing. (Isa. 10:27 KJV)*

Objects were anointed, too, when needed to bolster faith in an invisible God. God anointed Moses's rod when he complained (Exod. 4:2), Elijah's staff was anointed (2 Kings 4:29), Paul's handkerchiefs and aprons retained the anointing to heal diseases and cast out evil spirits (Acts 19:12), and even Peter's shadow was anointed (Act 5:15). God is able to do anything we can imagine, and more. By faith and prayer God's Spirit is mobilized (Zech. 4:6). The yolk shall be destroyed because of the anointing (Isa. 10:27).

There seems to be a pattern to the level and type of anointing God gives to mankind.

The first level is given when a person accepts Christ and the work He did on the cross. When a person wanted to enter into the Hebrew camp and become one of them in the Old Testament, there was a lepers ceremony that was performed (Lev. 14). It depicted Christ's suffering, death, and resurrection with the atoning blood and the anointing of the Holy Spirit. Entering into the camp is like entering into a relationship with Jesus today. We accept God's plan for our salvation and put ourselves under His authority. Jesus breathed on His apostles when they fully accepted Him as their Lord and Savior, and He said, "Receive the Holy Spirit" (John 20:22). All believers are given this level of the Holy Spirit for their own benefit (2 Cor. 1:21–23).

The second level of anointing is given as God wills and not based on works, but it does seem when a person daily fellowships with the Lord, reads the Word of God regularly, that God enables them to start blessing others. This is the priestly anointing. In the Old Testament, the priests had daily duties of trimming the lamps and performing sacrifices and the like for the spiritual needs of the people. The apostles might have received their priestly anointing at Pentecost (Acts 2:38). They were enabled by this anointing to serve others, and many were added to the church.

The third level (if there are levels) seems to be given for obedience. When one is obedient to God's will, even in adversity, God's enabling anointing of power is given. This is equivalent to the kingly anointing of the Old Testament. Kings had authority over many and dealt with other nations and countries (principalities and powers). The apostles received this kingly anointing in Acts 4:31–33 when they were given great power (dunamis). The result is recorded in Acts 5:12–15. Signs, wonders, and many added to the Lord!

For he whom God hath sent speaketh the words of God: for God giveth not the Spirit by measure unto him. The Father loveth the Son, and hath given all things into his hand. (John 3:34–35) KJV

And they withstood Uzziah the king, and said unto him, It appertaineth not unto thee, Uzziah, to burn incense unto the LORD, but to the priests the sons of Aaron, that are consecrated to burn incense: go out of the sanctuary; for thou hast trespassed; neither shall it be for thine honour from the LORD God. Then Uzziah was wroth, and had a censer in his hand to burn incense: and while he was wroth with the priests, the leprosy even rose up in his forehead before the priests in the house of the LORD, from beside the incense altar. And Azariah the chief priest, and all the priests, looked upon him, and, behold, he was leprous in his forehead, and they thrust him out from thence; yea, himself hasted also to go out, because the LORD had smitten him. And Uzziah the king was a leper unto the day of his death, and dwelt in a several house, being a leper; for he was cut off from the house of the LORD: and Jotham his son was over the king's house, judging the people of the land. (2 (Chron. 26:18–21 KJV)

And he tarried seven days, according to the set time that Samuel had appointed: but

Samuel came not to Gilgal; and the people were scattered from him. And Saul said, Bring hither a burnt offering to me, and peace offerings. And he offered the burnt offering. And it came to pass, that as soon as he had made an end of offering the burnt offering, behold, Samuel came; and Saul went out to meet him, that he might salute him. And Samuel said, What hast thou done? And Saul said, Because I saw that the people were scattered from me, and that thou camest not within the days appointed, and that the Philistines gathered themselves together at Michmash; Therefore said I, The Philistines will come down now upon me to Gilgal, and I have not made supplication unto the LORD: I forced myself therefore, and offered a burnt offering. And Samuel said to Saul, Thou hast done foolishly: thou hast not kept the commandment of the LORD thy God, which he commanded thee: for now would the LORD have established thy kingdom upon Israel forever. But now thy kingdom shall not continue: the LORD hath sought him a man after his own heart, and the LORD hath commanded him to be captain over his people, because thou hast not kept that which the LORD commanded thee. (1 Sam. 13:8–14 KJV)

The Holy Spirit Brings Spiritual Gifts

Since God is very smart, knowing the future, all powerful, and wants the best for each of us, He has a plan for every person according to His desires. To accomplish this plan, He gives us spiritual gifts when we receive the Holy Spirit. If we choose to follow His leading through life, we will experience not only great joy but also a feeling of great accomplishment. Paul described these gifts in 1 Corinthians chapter 12–14.

> *Now concerning spiritual gifts, brethren, I would not have you ignorant. Ye know that ye were Gentiles, carried away unto these dumb idols, even as ye were led. Wherefore I give you to understand, that no man speaking by the Spirit of God calleth Jesus accursed: and that no man can say that Jesus is the Lord, but by the Holy Ghost. Now there are diversities of gifts, but the same Spirit. And there are differences of administrations, but the same Lord. And there are diversities of operations, but it is the same God which worketh all in all. But the manifestation of the Spirit is given to every man to profit withal. For to one is given by the Spirit the word of wisdom; to another the word of knowledge by the same Spirit; To another faith by the same Spirit; to another the gifts of healing by the same Spirit; To another the working of miracles; to another prophecy; to another discerning of spirits; to another divers kinds of tongues; to another the interpretation of tongues: But*

all these worketh that one and the selfsame Spirit, dividing to every man severally as he will. For as the body is one, and hath many members, and all the members of that one body, being many, are one body: so also is Christ. For by one Spirit are we all baptized into one body, whether we be Jews or Gentiles, whether we be bond or free; and have been all made to drink into one Spirit. For the body is not one member, but many. If the foot shall say, Because I am not the hand, I am not of the body; is it therefore not of the body? And if the ear shall say, Because I am not the eye, I am not of the body; is it therefore not of the body? If the whole body were an eye, where were the hearing? If the whole were hearing, where were the smelling? But now hath God set the members every one of them in the body, as it hath pleased him. And if they were all one member, where were the body? But now are they many members, yet but one body. And the eye cannot say unto the hand, I have no need of thee: nor again the head to the feet, I have no need of you. Nay, much more those members of the body, which seem to be more feeble, are necessary: And those members of the body, which we think to be less honourable, upon these we bestow more abundant honour; and our uncomely parts have more abundant comeliness. For our comely parts have no need: but God hath tempered the body together, having given more abundant honour to that part which lacked: That there should be no schism in the body; but that the members should have the same care one for another. And whether one member suffer, all the members suffer with it; or one member be honoured, all the members rejoice with it. Now ye are the body of Christ, and members in particular. And God hath set some in the church, first apostles, secondarily prophets, thirdly teachers, after that miracles, then gifts of healings, helps, governments, diversities of tongues. Are all apostles? are all prophets? are all teachers? are all workers of miracles? Have all the gifts of healing? do all speak with tongues? do all interpret? But covet earnestly the best gifts: and yet show I unto you a more excellent way. (1 Cor. 12:1–31 KJV)

Though I speak with the tongues of men and of angels, and have not charity, I am become as sounding brass, or a tinkling cymbal. And though I have the gift of prophecy, and understand all mysteries, and all knowledge; and though I have all faith, so that I could remove mountains, and have not charity, I am nothing. And though I bestow all my goods to feed the poor, and though I give my body to be burned, and have not charity, it profiteth me nothing. Charity suffereth long, and is kind; charity envieth not; charity vaunteth not itself, is not puffed up, Doth not behave itself unseemly, seeketh not her own, is not easily provoked, thinketh no evil; Rejoiceth not in iniquity, but rejoiceth in the truth; Beareth all things, believeth all things, hopeth all things, endureth all things. Charity never faileth: but whether there be prophecies, they shall fail; whether there be tongues, they shall cease; whether there be knowledge, it shall vanish away. For we know in part, and we prophesy in part. But when that which is perfect is come, then that which is in part shall be done away. When I was a child, I spake as a child, I understood as a child, I thought as a child: but when I became a man, I put away childish things. For now we see through a glass, darkly; but then face to face: now I know in part; but then shall I know even as also I am known. And now abideth faith, hope, charity, these three; but the greatest of these is charity. (1 Cor. 13:1–13 KJV)

Follow after charity, and desire spiritual gifts, but rather that ye may prophesy. For he that speaketh in an unknown tongue speaketh not unto men, but unto God: for no man understandeth him; howbeit in the spirit he speaketh mysteries. But he that prophesieth speaketh unto men to edification, and exhortation, and comfort. He that speaketh in an unknown tongue edifieth himself; but he that prophesieth edifieth the church. (1 Cor. 14:1–4 KJV)

I believe that both speaking in tongues and prophecy still exists today, but not many people are asking God for these powerful gifts. There is great satisfaction in being able to communicate directly to God spirit to Spirit and to hear His voice within your heart. It promotes a deeper relationship and strengthens the partnership. Speaking in tongues starts out with a person verbalizing their prayer language, but as time goes by, with practice it becomes apparent that it is a waste of time running it through the brain and out the mouth. Your spirit has a voice of its own that communicates directly to God, which makes it possible to pray without ceasing. In fact, it is possible to be speaking to a person and to God at the same time. Many people experience this when praying for the sick and experience a passion or a burden in their hearts. Speaking in tongues keeps us humble and in tune with Holy Spirit and His desires instead of praying from our soulish desires or earthly experience.

Karis means "gift" in Greek, *ma* means "flowing" or "moving," and *ta* means "plural." Therefore, *Karismata* means "over flowing gifts."

God's overall plan for the world may resemble the stages of human life.

There is a pattern of seven all through the Bible, seven days of creation, seven days in a week, and two passages in scripture that says one thousand years is as one day to God. Some theologians believe that this age of man on earth is therefore seven thousand years. Stages of human life may correlate to the history of the human race. There seems to be a correlation between the seventy-year life span of a person and the seven-thousand-year history since the garden of Eden to the promised new heaven and earth.

Man/World	Man Shall Live 70 Yrs.	This Age Shall Last 7,000 Yrs.
Infant / Age of Innocence	When a person is first born, they are helpless and the parents do everything needed for them.	Age of innocence when Adam and Eve were in the garden of Eden. God took total care of them.
Early School / Age of Conscience	It doesn't take long for the child to start getting into trouble—the terrible twos! They rebel and want things their way. At 9–10 years old, the child has learned the family rules.	Adam and Eve sinned in the garden. They now learn how to work and take care of themselves. Adam lived to 970 years old.
Adolescence / Idolatry	The teen years bring on hero worship and teen idols. Allegiance issues arise.	So it was in the world when the earth was 1,300–1,600 years old. The world became so corrupt that God had to bring the flood in year 2349 BC.

Young Man / Age of Government	The young man starts experimenting with different vices. Alcohol, cigarettes, and drugs. Sin is taken too lightly, and a person risks getting hooked. Becomes marked.	After the flood, Noah experimented with making wine, resulting in Ham falling under a curse. Man rebelled against God at the Tower of Babel.
Young Adult / Age of Promise	A young man leaves home about age 20 to find his place in the world. He is not an instant success but starts building his life defining goals. He usually lives a worldly life until age 25.	When the earth was 2,000 years old, Abraham left home in search of his promised land. He didn't possess it instantly either. The sons of Jacob also rebelled and mistreated Joseph, ending up in Egyptian bondage in year 2100.

Mature Adult / Age of Law	At 25 a young man starts to settle down, look for a wife, and develop some morals that will lead to his success. He makes a marriage covenant with his wife and enters into his promised land. At age 34 there may be some bumps in the road of life—divorce, sickness, etc.	At year 2500, Moses got the Ten Commandments from God, and God calls Israel (His wife) and brings them to their promised land. In year 3300, the chosen people went into Assyrian captivity, and in 3400, Babylonian captivity.
Grace / Age of Grace	At age 40–60, a man reaches a turning point in his life. Either a midlife crisis or a higher road. For some, businesses expand as people become more productive.	When the Messiah came in 4000, Israel could accept or reject Him. They expected Jesus to get rid of the Romans and set up His kingdom. God instead expanded his business of saving souls.

Rest / Age of Rest	At 60, a person starts planning retirement and turning the family business over to the son. The next 10 years are resting and enjoying the fruit of a life of hard work.	God also rested the seventh day from His work and has promised his people a millennium of rest. He is turning the business over to Jesus.

The Mysteries of God's Plan Revealed in Christ

The path to understanding and living in the kingdom of God here on earth starts with building a foundation on Jesus Christ. He is the grace and glory of God (John 1:14). Glory is any good invasion of God into our lives, like healing, answered prayer, provision, or even feeling God's peace and presence. God has a good and perfect plan for each of our lives and gives us grace to perform it (Deut. 8–18; Eph. 1:3–4; 1 Cor. 3:10; Job 36:11; Jer. 29:11). We access God's grace by faith (Rom. 5:2), and we get faith by meditating on the Word of God (Rom. 10:17). Our words show our faith, and when they line up with God's Word, it activates the grace of God. Jesus says grace is like a perfect seed from God that needs to be planted deep into our hearts and be nurtured to grow (Mark 4:1–15; Rom 4:16–17).

Jesus tells us why people don't receive grace from God. The soil of our hearts won't allow the seed to grow, there are spiritual laws involved, we reap what we sow (a seed reproduces after its own kind), we are not patient to allow the seed to mature, no man can serve two masters, we don't ask God for help, and when we do ask, we ask for the wrong reasons, like greed or lust. We don't forgive ourselves and others, and we compromise worldly ways instead of godly concepts.

- The mystery of the seed (Mark 4:1–20)
- Mystery of the kingdom (Matt. 6:24–34)
- Mystery of the wild olive shoot (Rom. 11:17)

> *Therefore it is of faith, that it might be by grace; to the end the promise might be sure to all the seed; not to that only which is of the law, but to that also which is of the faith of Abraham; who is the father of us all, (As it is written, I have made thee a father of many nations,) before him whom he believed, even God, who quickeneth the dead, and calleth those things which be not as though they were. (Rom. 4:16–17 KJV)*

> *So then faith cometh by hearing, and hearing by the word of God. (Rom. 10:17 KJV)*

> *That the communication [speaking] of thy faith may become effectual [start working] by the acknowledging of every good thing which is in you in Christ Jesus. (Philem. 1:6 KJV)*

> *By whom also we have access by faith into this grace wherein we stand, and rejoice in hope of the glory of God. And not only so, but we*

glory in tribulations also: knowing that tribulation worketh patience; And patience, experience; and experience, hope: And hope maketh not ashamed; because the love of God is shed abroad in our hearts by the Holy Ghost which is given unto us. (Rom. 5:2–5 KJV)

If they obey and serve him, they shall spend their days in prosperity, and their years in pleasures. (Job 36:11 KJV)

For I know the thoughts that I think toward you, saith the Lord, thoughts of peace, and not of evil, to give you an expected end. (Jer. 29:11 KJV)

I do not want you to be ignorant of this mystery, brothers, so that you may not be conceited: Israel has experienced a hardening in part until the full number of the Gentiles has come in. And so all Israel will be saved, as it is written. (Rom. 11:25 KJV)

Now to him who is able to establish you by my gospel and the proclamation of Jesus Christ, according to the revelation of the mystery hidden for long ages past, but now revealed and made known through the prophetic writings by the command of the eternal God, so that all nations might believe and obey him—to the only wise God be glory forever through Jesus Christ! Amen. (Rom. 16:25 KJV)

But we speak the wisdom of God in a mystery, even the hidden wisdom, which God ordained before the world unto our glory: Which none of the princes of this world knew: for had they known it, they would not have crucified the Lord of glory. But as it is written, Eye hath not seen, nor ear heard, neither have entered into the heart of man, the things which God hath prepared for them that love him. But God hath revealed them unto us by his Spirit: for the Spirit searcheth all things, yea, the deep things of God. (1 Cor. 2:7–10 KJV)

Light versus Darkness

God calls Himself light in the Bible.

We have examined the two different kinds of light discussed in the Bible. We are all familiar with the light from the sun and stars that are sources of light, and the moon that reflects light, but there is another light from God and is often equated to His glory or knowledge. Below, find more about light.

This then is the message which we have heard of him, and declare unto you, that God is light, and in him is no darkness at all. (1 John 1:5 KJV)

And the city had no need of the sun, neither of the moon, to shine in it: for the glory of

God did lighten it, and the Lamb is the light thereof. (Rev. 21:23 KJV)

For God, who commanded the light to shine out of darkness, hath shined in our hearts, to give the light of the knowledge of the glory of God in the face of Jesus Christ. (2 Cor. 4:6 KJV)

The first thing God created on the first day was light, spelled "OWR" in the Hebrew language. God said literally, "Ye-hee Owr," which is "Me come into existence."

Then God said, "Let there be light"; and there was light. And God saw that the light was good; and God separated the light from the darkness. God called the light Day, and the darkness he called Night. And there was evening and there was morning, the first day. (Gen. 1:3 KJV)

The Hebrew word for *light* in Genesis 1:3 is *owr*, pronounced "ore," from *Strong's Concordance* H215, root word *illumination* or (concr.) *enlightenment* (in every sense, including lightning, happiness, etc.): bright, clear, plus day, light (the Glory of God).

All things were made by him; and without him was not anything made that was made. In him was life; and the life was the light of men. And the light shineth in darkness; and the darkness comprehended it not. There was a man sent from God, whose name was

John. The same came for a witness, to bear witness of the Light, that all men through him might believe. He was not that Light, but was sent to bear witness of that Light. That was the true Light, which lighteth every man that cometh into the world. He was in the world, and the world was made by him, and the world knew him not. (John 1:3–10 KJV)

Later, on the fourth day, God created the sun, moon, and stars to shed another kind of light on the earth.

And God said, Let there be lights in the firmament of the heaven to divide the day from the night; and let them be for signs, and for seasons, and for days, and years: And let them be for lights in the firmament of the heaven to give light upon the earth: and it was so. And God made two great lights; the greater light to rule the day, and the lesser light to rule the night: he made the stars also. And God set them in the firmament of the heaven to give light upon the earth, And to rule over the day and over the night, and to divide the light from the darkness: and God saw that it was good. And the evening and the morning were the fourth day. (Gen. 1:14–19 KJV)

The *light* in Genesis 1:14 is spelled different than in Genesis 1:3 in the Hebrew language. Refer to *Strong's Concordance* item 3974. In Genesis 1:14 it is spelled *maw-*

ore', or *ma'or, maw-ore'*; also (in plural) fem. me'owrah, meh-o-raw'; or me'orah, meh-o-raw'; from H215; prop. a luminous body or luminary, i.e. (abstr.) light (as an element); fig. brightness, i.e., spec. a chandelier: bright, light. (sun, moon and stars)

Energy in a light beam is affected by the media the light travels through. Some light is reflected, some absorbed, and some passes through the media. Eyeglasses are a good example. An antireflective coating is often put on the lenses to minimize the reflective energy loss, and the lens material is selected to minimize the absorption loss to allow more light to the eye. Likewise, the invisible God is reflected off the church to those in the vicinity and the blessings of God absorbed by the church members. Jesus said we are a light on a hill that cannot be hidden.

White light is made up of the addition of all colors or frequencies. The separate frequencies of light can be split out to their separate colors. The attributes of light from our sun correlate somewhat to creation.

Rainbow Colors Correlate to the Days of Creation

Six Days of Creation and Then Rest

- Violet = Royal or light of God (glory)
- Blue = Waters
- Green = Grass
- Yellow = Sun, moon, and stars
- Orange = Cold-blooded animals
- Red = Adam and warm-blooded mammals
- Infrared = Day of rest

The Pattern of the Menorah

The menorah stood as a symbol of light in a dark place. It is a large candlestick on the left side of the holy place in the tabernacle as a person enters. It has seven oil lamps, of which the center lamp is the tallest and is called the servant lamp because all the other lamps are lit from it. The scriptures are full of the pattern of seven, and most patterns of seven are divided into three plus four. Often, the central idea is the fourth item of the pattern of seven and usually deals with the battle of light versus darkness (good versus evil).

The battle between light and darkness, symbolized by the number 4.

For example, in Revelation:

- Fourth seal, pale horse = death and hell darkness (Rev. 6:7–8)
- Fourth trumpet = sun, moon, and stars smitten (Rev. 8:12)
- Fourth sign = 144,000 evangelists enlighten the world (Rev. 14:1)
- Fourth vial = wrath poured out on the sun (Rev. 16:8)
- Fourth sight = New Jerusalem doesn't need light (Rev. 21:2)

God's fourth visit to Abraham in Genesis 15:12, there was darkness until the fullness of evil, followed by blessing in Genesis 22:17.

There were seven sayings Jesus spoke on the cross in the six hours (9:00 a.m. to 3:00 p.m.). The sun became dark between 12:00 p.m. and 3:00 p.m. The fourth thing Jesus said on the cross as the sun went dark for three hours starting at noon, "My God, my God, why hast thou forsaken me?" Maybe He was experiencing and paying the price for our sins at this time.

Christ may have died for all of mankind through each time era:

Adam	(1) "Father forgive them for they know not what they do" (Luke 23:34).
Noah	(2) "Thou shalt be with me in paradise" (Luke 23:43).
Sinai	(3) "My God, my God why hast thou forsaken me?" (Matt. 27:46).
Light vs Dark	(4) "Woman, behold thy son" (John 19:26).
Church	(5) "I thirst" (John 19:28).
Last Millennia	(6) "It is finished" (John 19:30).
New Earth.	(7) "Father into thy hands I commend my spirit" (Luke 23:46).

Jesus entered into rest. His work was finished on the cross in Jerusalem and relating to the end of the millennium where evil ends.

This light seems to be more than just light. It is God's illumination and includes wisdom and understanding. It seems to be part of Himself.

The glory is God's light.

> *And the city had no need of the sun, neither of the moon, to shine in it: for the glory of God did lighten it, and the Lamb is the light thereof. (Rev. 21:23 KJV)*

And he carried me away in the spirit to a great and high mountain, and showed me that great city, the holy Jerusalem, descending out of heaven from God, Having the glory of God: and her light was like unto a stone most precious. (Rev. 21:10–11 KJV)

Relationships and Patterns

There is one glory of the sun, and another glory of the moon, and another glory of the stars: for one star differeth from another star in glory. So also is the resurrection of the dead. It is sown in corruption; it is raised in incorruption: It is sown in dishonour; it is raised in glory: it is sown in weakness; it is raised in power: It is sown a natural body; it is raised a spiritual body. There is a natural body, and there is a spiritual body. And so it is written, The first man Adam was made a living soul; the last Adam was made a quickening spirit. Howbeit that was not first which is spiritual, but that which is natural; and afterward that which is spiritual. The first man is of the earth, earthy: the second man is the Lord from heaven. (1 Cor. 15:41–47 KJV)

I form the light, and create darkness: I make peace, and create evil: I the LORD do all these things. (Isa. 45:7 KJV)

Ye are all the children of light, and the children of the day: we are not of the night, nor of darkness. Therefore let us not sleep, as do others; but let us watch and be sober. (1 Thess. 5:5–6 KJV)

(Jesus) Who is the image of the invisible God, the firstborn of every creature: For by him were all things created, that are in heaven, and that are in earth, visible and invisible, whether they be thrones, or dominions, or principalities, or powers: all things were created by him, and for him: And he is before all things, and by him all things consist. (Col. 1:15–17 KJV)

Then spake Jesus again unto them, saying, I am the light of the world: he that followeth me shall not walk in darkness, but shall have the light of life. (John 8:12 KJV)

Then Jesus said unto them, Yet a little while is the light with you. Walk while ye have the light, lest darkness come upon you: for he that walketh in darkness knoweth not whither he goeth. While ye have light, believe in the light, that ye may be the children of light. (John 12:35–36 KJV)

Webster defines *light* as (1) electromagnetic waves that travel 186,270 miles per second, (2) radiant energy that acts on the retina of the eye, and (3) knowledge, information, illumination of the mind.

Scientists don't really know what light is. It travels through space and is invisible until it is reflected off some substance. It acts both like a particle and a wave. It hums at different frequencies to generate different colors. May I suggest that God is invisible unless He is reflected off us? Jesus said He was the light of the world and later said we were the light of the world and a city on a hill.

Darkness is the absence of light.

People perish for lack of Knowledge. (Hosea 4:6 KJV)

Then God said, "Let there be light"; and there was light. And God saw that the light was good; and God separated the light from the darkness. God called the light Day, and the darkness he called Night. And there was evening and there was morning, the first day. (Gen. 1:3–5 KJV)

How art thou fallen from heaven, O Lucifer, son of the morning! how art thou cut down to the ground, which didst weaken the nations! For thou hast said in thine heart, I will ascend into heaven, I will exalt my throne above the stars of God: I will sit also upon the mount of the congregation, in the sides of the north: I will ascend above the heights of the clouds: I will be like the most High. (Isa. 14:12–14 KJV)

When the morning stars sang together, and all the sons of God shouted for joy? (Job 38:7 KJV)

Moreover the word of the LORD came unto me, saying, Son of man, take up a lamentation upon the king of Tyrus, and say unto him, Thus saith the Lord GOD; Thou sealest up the sum, full of wisdom, and perfect in beauty. Thou hast been in Eden the garden of God; every precious stone was thy covering, the sardius, topaz, and the diamond, the beryl, the onyx, and the jasper, the sapphire, the emerald, and the carbuncle, and gold: the workmanship of thy tabrets and of thy pipes was prepared in thee in the day that thou wast created. Thou art the anointed cherub that covereth; and I have set thee so: thou wast upon the holy mountain of God; thou hast walked up and down in the midst of the stones of fire. Thou wast perfect in thy ways from the day that thou wast created, till iniquity was found in thee. (Ezek. 28:11–15 KJV)

And the great dragon was cast out, that old serpent, called the Devil, and Satan, which deceives the whole world: he was cast out into the earth, and his angels were cast out with him. (Rev. 12:9 KJV)

For we wrestle not against flesh and blood, but against principalities, against powers, against the rulers of the darkness of this world, against spiritual wickedness in high places. (Eph. 6:12 KJV)

False Illumination of Satan

Our enemy, Satan, tries to take the place of Christ through three tactics: (1) deception, where he tries to get us to believe a lie; (2) division, where he wants to divide people; and (3) destruction.

For such are false apostles, deceitful workers, transforming themselves into the apostles of Christ. And no marvel; for Satan himself is transformed into an angel of light. (Cor. 11:13–14 KJV)

There shall not be found among you any one that maketh his son or his daughter to pass through the fire, or that useth divination, or an observer of times, or an enchanter, or a witch, Or a charmer, or a consulter with familiar spirits, or a wizard, or a necromancer. For all that do these things are an abomination unto the LORD. (Deut. 18:10–12 KJV)

And this is the condemnation, that light is come into the world, and men loved darkness rather than light, because their deeds were evil. (John 3:18 KJV)

More about Spiritual Warfare

The three battlegrounds are Satan, the world, and the flesh.

Satan

Put on the whole armour of God, that ye may be able to stand against the wiles of the devil. For we wrestle not against flesh and blood, but against principalities, against powers, against the rulers of the darkness of this world, against spiritual wickedness in high places. (Eph. 6:11–12 KJV)

World

Love not the world, neither the things that are in the world. If any man loves the world, the love of the Father is not in him. For all that is in the world, the lust of the flesh, and the lust of the eyes, and the pride of life, is not of the Father, but is of the world. And the world passeth away, and the lust thereof: but he that doeth the will of God abideth forever. (1 John 2:15–17 KJV)

Flesh

This I say then, Walk in the Spirit, and ye shall not fulfil the lust of the flesh. For the flesh lusteth against the Spirit, and the Spirit against the flesh: and these are con-

trary the one to the other: so that ye cannot do the things that ye would. But if ye be led of the Spirit, ye are not under the law. Now the works of the flesh are manifest, which are these; Adultery, fornication, uncleanness, lasciviousness, Idolatry, witchcraft, hatred, variance, emulations, wrath, strife, seditions, heresies, Envyings, murders, drunkenness, revellings, and such like: of the which I tell you before, as I have also told you in time past, that they which do such things shall not inherit the kingdom of God. (Gal. 5:16–21 KJV)

The tools God gives us: the name of Jesus against Satan, crucify fleshly (self-centered) desires, resist evil, knowing the blood of Jesus covers sin.

It is God's plan to give mankind authority over Satan and his minions.

Attitudes of the Nations

Bondage

God reveals the tactics of the enemy, Satan, through the stories of the Old Testament. Each nation that the children of Israel contacted fought against God's plans in various ways. Egypt had a spirit of bondage. They put Israel into slavery, murdered innocent children by throwing them into the Nile River, and put taskmasters over them that controlled them for the profit of Egypt. In the USA, we see a shadow of the same thing in the abortion of innocent babies for convenience, and overtaxation, which keeps people in poverty.

Division

Assyria had a spirit of division. They divided Israel's northern tribes from the southern tribes. We see a residue of this repeating here in the US, where the north and south were divided, which led to the War Between the States. Even now, there is an attitude difference between the Northern states and the Southern states. God says we should seek unity, forgiving one another.

Compromise

Babylon had a spirit of compromise. In Babylon, Daniel was asked to eat meat offered to idols to compromise his faith in God. He was told not to pray, but he threw open his window so all could see and prayed anyway. Daniel refused to bow down to the golden idol and compromise his faith in God. The US has experienced this same spirit in the form of other religious concepts and ideas that are dangled in front of Christian believers. "A little white lie is acceptable in some circumstances," for example. The enemy would have us believe that all religions are good and lead to salvation, which is a lie. There is only one God and one path to salvation.

Antichrist

The Meads/Persians had a spirit of the antichrist. The definition of *antichrist* is "instead of" not "against." The story of Ester parallels Revelation, where God's chosen are saved and Satan is thrown into the lake of fire. Ester is a shadow of

Christianity and Hamon, a type of antichrist. The ten kings are a symbol of the ten nations in Revelation.

Philosophy

The Greeks had a spirit of philosophy. Eager to hear something new and quoting learned men of their time whose teachings often contradict God's truth. Always learning but never accepting truth. The US has scholarly teachers in universities that teach that believing in God is old-fashioned, a crutch that shows weakness, etc. They resist the pure knowledge of God and often mock Christian believers who believe what God says about creation.

Tolerance

The Romans had a spirit of tolerance. They tolerated all gods of all nations except Christians, whom they fed to the lions. God turned it around at the end when many Romans turned and Christianity became the religion of Rome. This tolerance of other gods can be seen today in the agenda of the new world order: one world with one religion getting along, like one big happy family. Believing there are many pathways to God and thus accepting other doctrines. Finding tolerance and common ground, so to speak, sounds great, but is not God's plan. Our God will not share His Godhead with other gods.

God's plan is to give authority to believers.

> *And he said unto them, I beheld Satan as lightning fall from heaven. Behold, I give unto you power to tread on serpents and scorpions, and over all the power of the*

enemy: and nothing shall by any means hurt you. Notwithstanding in this rejoice not, that the spirits are subject unto you; but rather rejoice, because your names are written in heaven. (Luke 10:18 KJV)

A Roman centurion understood authority and told Jesus to just say the word and his servant would be healed over a distance of nineteen miles. Jesus is amazed at his understanding of authority and his faith.

And when Jesus was entered into Capernaum, there came unto him a centurion, beseeching him, And saying, Lord, my servant lieth at home sick of the palsy, grievously tormented. And Jesus saith unto him, I will come and heal him. The centurion answered and said, Lord, I am not worthy that thou should come under my roof: but speak the word only, and my servant shall be healed. For I am a man under authority, having soldiers under me: and I say to this man, Go, and he goeth; and to another, Come, and he cometh; and to my servant, Do this, and he doeth it. When Jesus heard it, he marvelled, and said to them that followed, Verily I say unto you, I have not found so great faith, no, not in Israel. And I say unto you, That many shall come from the east and west, and shall sit down with Abraham, and Isaac, and Jacob, in the kingdom of heaven. But the children of the kingdom shall be cast out into outer dark-

ness: there shall be weeping and gnashing of teeth. And Jesus said unto the centurion, Go thy way; and as thou hast believed, so be it done unto thee. And his servant was healed in the selfsame hour. (Matt. 8:5–13 KJV)

When Adam and Eve sinned, Satan obtained power and authority on earth (Gen. 1:26), but the work Jesus did on the cross transferred all power and authority to Him. He has passed this power and authority to His disciples and to believers. Let God's will be done on earth as it is in heaven.

Then he called his twelve disciples together, and gave them power and authority over all devils, and to cure diseases. And he sent them to preach the kingdom of God, and to heal the sick. (Luke 9:1–2 KJV)

And Jesus came to them and spake unto them, saying, All authority hath been given unto me in heaven and on earth. Go ye therefore, and make disciples of all the nations, baptizing them into the name of the Father and of the Son and of the Holy Spirit: teaching them to observe all things whatsoever I commanded you: and lo, I am with you always, even unto the end of the world. (Matt. 28:18–20 KJV)

And he said unto them, Go ye into all the world, and preach the gospel to the whole creation. He that believeth and is baptized shall be saved; but he that disbelieveth shall be condemned. And these signs shall accompany them that believe: in my name shall they cast out demons; they shall speak with new tongues; they shall take up serpents, and if they drink any deadly thing, it shall in no wise hurt them; they shall lay hands on the sick, and they shall recover. So then the Lord Jesus, after he had spoken unto them, was received up into heaven, and sat down at the right hand of God. And they went forth, and preached everywhere, the Lord working with them, and confirming the word by the signs that followed. Amen. (Mark 16:15–20 KJV)

Our part is to take authority over the works of Satan and God alone, working with us—heals the sick, converts a soul, or delivers a person from Satan's bondage. Those that put themselves under the authority of God have authority in God. It is encouraging to know that Jesus put down His deity and operated as a man anointed by the Holy Spirit and shows us how we can do the same.

God has given mankind free will and dominion here on earth and usually does not operate here without permission. God said He would consult His prophets before doing anything, and Moses even got Him to change His mind when He wanted to kill everyone when they made the golden calf. Even the birth of Christ was prayed for by mankind before it came to pass.

Conclusion

The main theme of the entire Bible is about the salvation of mankind presented in many different ways—stories of people, symbology, patterns, types, allegories, and God's contractual promises. Each believer is given His Holy Spirit with gifts to help them grow and mature. The steps of growing and maturing spiritually is called sanctification. Each person has a different path but will include receiving the Holy Spirit, receiving gifts and provisions, receiving authority, and learning to resist evil on the three battlefields of life.

In the next chapter, we will look at the definitions of the church, basic Christian beliefs, and some of the tools God provides for us to operate as Christians. We will see how to hear the voice of God and stay strong in Christ.

CHAPTER 5

How Is Mankind to Function as Christians?

Salvation is joining God's family, going to heaven for eternity, and escaping the agony of hell for eternity. It comes by believing and accepting God's plan of salvation, where Jesus died on the cross for the sins of the world and was resurrected the third day. By believing and declaring the work of Christ on the cross, we join God's family. Just as the Hebrews were saved and delivered out of Egypt by believing God's Word was true. They applied the blood of a lamb on their doorposts, ate the lamb dinner, and prepared to move out of Egypt in the morning. After they left Egypt came the walk in the desert for forty years, where God fed them and taught them of His law, His attributes, and His characteristics. As new Christians, we go through life in a similar fashion, called sanctification, where God feeds us spiritual food and teaches us spiritual truths. For example, we learn to respect the people around us who are made in the image of God and the new covenant principles, such as humility, love, and grace. God puts His law within our hearts, and we choose to become Christlike in our spirit. We are born carnal into this world, and we are born spiritually into heaven after choosing the truth and receiving God's plan of salvation. God gives us an engagement ring in the form of the Holy Spirit, with a promise of marriage in the future. Jesus has now gone away to prepare a place for us in heaven and will return for us at His second coming at the end of the age. The process of sanctification is God's work as we grow and become Christlike through our submission and the work of the Holy Spirit. The Hebrews finally crossed over the Jordan River to the promised land but still had to fight to overcome the land of milk and honey, and likewise, Christians cross over into a more fruitful life partnered with God, but we still have to fight evil. Peter describes this process of sanctification in 1 Peter 1:5:

> But also for this very reason, giving all diligence, add to your faith virtue, to virtue knowledge, to knowledge self-control, to self-control perseverance, to perseverance godliness, to godliness brotherly kindness, and to brotherly kindness love. For if these things are yours and abound, you will be neither barren nor unfruitful in the knowledge of our Lord Jesus Christ. For he who lacks these things is shortsighted, even to blindness, and has forgotten that he was cleansed from his old sins. (1 Pet. 1:5–9 KJV)

Notice that these things are all spiritual gifts or fruits offered by God. We must be awake enough to ask and accept them.

Gifts, Fruits, and Attitudes

There are other fruits and attitudes discussed in the Bible that are part of the sanctification process. We are defined by our identity, ability, and purpose. The following is a summary of some of these:

Gifts of the Spirit (1 Cor. 12:4–9)	Attitudes of the Spirit (Matt. 5)	Fruits of the Spirit (Gal. 5:22)
The word of wisdom	Humble	Love
The word of knowledge	Empathetic, mournful	Joy
Faith	Meek	Peace
Healings	Righteous	Long-suffering
Miracles	Merciful	Gentleness
Prophecy	Pure in Heart	Goodness
Discerning of Spirits	Peacemaking	Faith
Different Tongues	Persecuted	Meekness
Interpretation of Tongues	Suffering for gospel	Temperance

The gifts of Holy Spirit that God gives to the believers can be divided into three groups of three. Our words come from our heart or spirit; and therefore, the speaking gift of prophecy, speaking in tongues and interpretation of tongues, is for our spirit. Our soul is where our personality and knowledge reside; and therefore, the gift of knowledge, wisdom and discerning of spirits, is for our soul. The last three gifts are for our body where we do things. We are to lay hands on the sick for healing, exercise faith, and do workings of miracles by trusting in God.

Even the Lord's Prayer is divided into three to address the Godhead:

- "Our father who art in heaven" is to the Father.
- "Give us our daily bread and forgive" is to Jesus.
- "Deliver us from evil for thine is the power" is to the Holy Spirit.

Our calling gives us identity. We are told to be "holy" and be a "royal priesthood."

Our giftings give us ability (1 Pet. 4:10).

Our anointing gives us purpose and direction (Isa. 61).

> But ye [are] a chosen generation, a royal priesthood, an holy nation, a peculiar people; that ye should shew forth the praises of him who hath called you out of darkness into his marvelous light. (1 Pet. 2:9 KJV)

> Ye also, as lively stones, are built up a spiritual house, an holy priesthood, to offer up spiritual sacrifices, acceptable to God by Jesus Christ. (1 Pet. 2:5 KJV)

> According as each hath received a gift, ministering it among yourselves, as good stewards of the manifold grace of God. (1 Pet. 4:10)

The Spirit of the Lord GOD [is] upon me; because the LORD hath anointed me to preach good tidings unto the meek; he hath sent me to bind up the brokenhearted, to proclaim liberty to the captives, and the opening of the prison to [them that are] bound. (Ps. 61:1 KJV)

For the gifts and calling of God [are] without repentance. (Rom. 11:29 KJV)

For ye see your calling, brethren, how that not many wise men after the flesh, not many mighty, not many noble, [are called]. (1 Chron. 1:26 KJV)

Let every man abide in the same calling wherein he was called. (1 Chron. 7:20 KJV)

Who hath saved us, and called [us] with an holy calling, not according to our works, but according to his own purpose and grace, which was given us in Christ Jesus before the world began. (2 Tim. 1:9 KJV)

But the anointing which ye have received of him abideth in you, and ye need not that any man teach you: but as the same anointing teacheth you of all things, and is truth, and is no lie, and even as it hath taught you, ye shall abide in him. (1 John 2:27 KJV)

> *I counsel thee to buy of me gold tried in the fire, that thou mayest be rich; and white raiment, that thou mayest be clothed, and [that] the shame of thy nakedness does not appear; and anoint thine eyes with eye salve, that thou mayest see. (Rev. 3:18 KJV)*

Believer Symbology

The Fish Symbol

Fish live in a different realm (underwater), and Jesus lives in a different realm in heaven. Even though we are not physically in heaven yet, Jesus said we are seated in heavenly places spiritually and we can operate from there by living as Jesus did from our spirit here on earth. In this way, the fish is a good symbol of a Christian.

The Vine Symbol

"I am the Vine; you are the branches. The one who remains in Me and I in him bears much fruit, for [otherwise] apart from Me [that is, cut off from vital union with Me] you can do nothing" (John 15:5 AMP).

The Sheep Symbol

Christians are followers of Jesus, the Good Shepherd, and are therefore symbolized as sheep. Sheep have a loving, peaceful attitude and follow the shepherd, unlike the goats that are stubborn and contrary. Jesus said that His sheep hear His voice and follow Him.

The Lamp Symbol

Christians burn in their hearts with the gospel of truth, shedding light (knowledge) to a dying people, hoping to turn some to Christ for eternal life and joy.

The Seed Symbol

The Christian works in the fields of the earth, planting the seed of truth into the hearts of mankind, watering with the Word of God, and nurturing the tender shoots to maturity.

The Church Symbolized as the Human Body

The body metaphor for the people of God is a powerful image that symbolizes the new historical reality brought about in Christ. It surfaces in only four New Testament epistles, but in a bewildering array of associations (See 1 Cor. 12:27 and Eph. 4:12).

The Christian Church

After God calls us out of the world to Himself, we usually find ourselves joining a church where we can fellowship with God through worship and fellowship with one another. It is a safe place where Christians can learn about God and God can develop His children.

The *Christian Church* is an ecclesiological term generally used by Protestants to refer to the whole group of people belonging to Christianity throughout the history of Christianity. In this understanding, Christian Church does not refer to a particular Christian denomination but to the body of all believers. Some Christian traditions, however, believe that the term *Christian Church* or *church* applies only to a specific historic Christian body or institution (e.g., the Catholic Church, the Eastern Orthodox Church, the Oriental Orthodox Churches, or the Assyrian Church of the East). The four marks of the church, first expressed in the Nicene Creed, are that the church is one (a unified body of particular churches in full communion of doctrines and faith with one another), holy (a sanctified and deified body), Catholic (universal and containing the fullness of truth in itself), and apostolic (its hierarchy, doctrines, and faith can be traced back to the apostles).

Most English translations of the New Testament generally use the word *church* as a translation of the Ancient Greek ἐκκλησία, *ecclesia*, found in the original Greek texts, which generally meant an "assembly." This term appears in two verses of the gospel of Matthew, twenty-four verses in Acts of the Apostles, fifty-eight verses in Pauline epistles (including the earliest instances of its use in relation to a Christian body), two verses of the Letter to the Hebrews, one verse in the Epistle of James, three verses in the Third Epistle of John, and nineteen verses in the book of Revelation. In total, ἐκκλησία appears in the New Testament text 114 times, although not every instance is a technical reference to the church.

In the New Testament, the term ἐκκλησία is used for local communities as well as in a universal sense to mean all believers. Traditionally, only orthodox believers are considered part of the true church, but convictions of what is orthodox have long varied, as many churches (not only the ones officially using the term *orthodox* in their names) consider themselves to be orthodox and other Christians to be heterodox.

Sacraments of the Church

A *sacrament* is a Christian rite recognized as of particular importance and significance. There are various views on the existence and meaning of such rites. Many Christians consider the sacraments to be a visible symbol of the reality of God, as well as a means by which God enacts His grace. The seven accepted sacraments are thus:

1. Baptism
2. Confirmation
3. Holy Eucharist
4. Penance
5. Anointing of the Sick
6. Holy Orders
7. Matrimony

The church itself is a sacrament instituted by Christ to give grace and protection from the world. Jesus gave us his body, the church, to continue the works He performed during His earthly life. Grace given to us through the sacraments will help us lead a good life in this world and help save us for the kingdom of heaven.

The sacraments were instituted by Christ and were part of the tradition of the early Christian Church. The church celebrates in her liturgy the paschal *mystery* of Christ, his passion, sacrifice on the cross, resurrection, and glorious ascension. The Greek word μυστήριον, or *mystery* in the Greek New Testament, is translated into *sacramentum* in the Latin Vulgate Bible, from which we derive our English word *sacrament* (examples: Eph. 1:9; Eph. 3:9; Col. 1:27). The saving effects of Christ's redemption on the cross are communicated through the sacraments, especially in the liturgical celebration of the Eucharist. The sacraments to this day are called *mysteries* in the Eastern churches.

Catholic as well as Eastern Orthodox Churches all recognize the seven sacraments of baptism, confirmation, Holy Eucharist, penance, the anointing of the sick, holy orders, and matrimony. The three sacraments of Christian initiation are baptism, confirmation, and the Eucharist. The two sacraments of healing are penance and the anointing of the sick, and the two sacraments of vocation are holy orders and marriage. Three sacraments, baptism, confirmation, and holy orders, are given once, as they render a permanent seal or character upon one's soul (2 Cor. 1:21–22, Eph. 4:30, Rev. 7:3).

Each sacrament consists of a visible external rite, which is composed of *matter* and *form*, the matter being the action, such as the pouring of water in baptism, and the form being the words spoken by the minister. Each sacramental rite confers a special ecclesial effect and sacramental grace appropriate for each sacrament. The sacraments occur at pivotal events and give meaning to a person's life.

Grace

Grace is a favor, the free and undeserved gift from God through Christ Jesus, to help us respond to His call to become children of God, to become partakers of the divine nature and of eternal life. Our justification comes from the grace of God. Grace is a participation in the life of God and is necessary for salvation.

Worship

Worship is an act of religious devotion usually directed toward a deity (Wikipedia).

Definition of worship (in spirit and truth):

1. To honor or show reverence for as a divine being or supernatural power.
2. To regard with great or extravagant respect, honor, or devotion.

In Christianity, worship is the act of attributing reverent honor and homage to God. In the New Testament, various words are used to refer to the term *worship*.

In Christianity, a church service is a formalized period of communal worship, often but not exclusively occurring on Sunday (or on Saturday in the case of those churches practicing seventh-day Sabbatarianism). The church service is the gathering together of Christians to be taught the Word of God (the Holy Bible) and be encouraged in their faith. Technically, the "church" in "church service" refers to the gathering of the faithful rather than to the building in which the event takes place. In Christianity, worship is reverent honor and homage paid to God. The New Testament uses various words to express the concept of worship. The word *proskuneo*, "to worship," means to bow down.

Mass

Mass is the central act of divine worship in the Catholic Church. The Congregation for Divine Worship at the Vatican publishes a *Directory on Popular Piety and the Liturgy*. Roman

Catholic devotions are "external practices of piety" that are not part of the official liturgy of the Catholic Church but are part of the popular spiritual practices of Catholics. They do not become part of liturgical worship, even if conducted in a Catholic church, in a group, in the presence of a priest.

Anglican devotions are private prayers and practices used by Anglican Christians to promote spiritual growth and communion with God. Among members of the Anglican Communion, private devotional habits vary widely, depending on personal preference and on affiliation with low church or parishes. Forms of worship express who God is and our love toward Him.

Prayer

In Matthew chapter 6, Jesus outlines what not to do when you pray to God and what you should do for your prayers to be heard, as recorded in Romans 8:26–27 and Ephesians 6:18. Prayer is not for someone to get attention and impress other people or repeating a mantra over and over or even describing your problem to an all-knowing God. God already knows what we need before we ask. The pattern of prayer should match that of the Lord's Prayer, where the full Godhead is addressed. The Father in heaven is addressed (love and thanksgiving), the Son is addressed ("Give us this day our daily bread" and the like), and the Holy Spirit is addressed ("Lead us not into temptation"). Most Christians aren't aware that there are several types of prayer discussed in God's Word, and if you use one type when you should be using another, it may not work as well. You would be applying the wrong spiritual tool to your needs or request. Mixing worldly ideas with godly ideas is called compromise and may block prayer. Another problem that mankind has that may block prayer is unforgiveness. When we pray to God the Father, Jesus functions as the mediator and the Holy Spirit helps by interpreting our prayer. God may have intended for each of the six forms of prayer mentioned in the Bible to have different functions, as described below.

The Prayer of Agreement

In Matthew 18:19 (NKJV), Jesus introduced the prayer of agreement when He said, "Again I say to you that if two of you agree on earth concerning anything that they ask, it will be done for them by My Father in heaven."

Right off the bat you can see that for the prayer of agreement to work, the people involved in the prayer have to agree! You cannot know what someone else wants, what someone is believing for, and God cannot answer your prayer for someone else against his or her will. To use the prayer of agreement, you must be sure that the person with whom you are agreeing is in line with what you are asking for.

The Prayer of Faith

The prayer of faith, also known as petition prayer, is the prayer that most people think of when they use the term *prayer*. Petition prayer is between you and God. It is you asking God for a particular outcome.

The key verse for the prayer of faith is Mark 11:24 (KJV): "Therefore I say to you, whatever things you ask when you pray, believe that you receive them, and you will have them."

The rule to consider here is, the moment that you pray, you must believe that you receive what you asked for.

Now faith is the substance of things hoped for, the evidence of things not seen. Your faith is substance, something tangible. It is evidence of things you cannot see. (Heb. 11:1 KJV)

Notice that Mark 11:24 does not say when you will actually see the result of your prayer. It does not tell you how long it will take for that prayer result to appear, and this is where many Christians get hung up.

God lives in one eternal now. There is no past or present for Him. But we are temporal beings who live in the context of time.

When you pray in faith, God immediately gives you what you prayed for, in the spirit realm. But in the natural world, due to a number of factors, it may take time for the answer to manifest itself.

God answers prayers, and He will answer your specific prayer in line with His Word, but it is your faith that brings that answer out of the spiritual world and into the physical world. How many times in Scripture does Jesus say to someone, "According to your faith"?

He referred to people's faith constantly, and even though it was His power that healed them, He always credited their faith with being the catalyst. In fact, when Jesus went to His hometown, we are told that "He did not do many mighty works there because of their unbelief" (Matt. 13:58).

Did Jesus suddenly lose His power on that visit to Nazareth? No!

His power never changed. What changed? It was the people's level of faith mixed with His power.

There is a simple spiritual explanation for this. God will not do something against your will. God cannot violate free will. If you don't have faith to do something, He won't arbitrarily override your lack of faith.

The Prayer of Consecration and Dedication

In Luke 22:41–42 (KJV), "Father, if it is Your will, take this cup away from Me; nevertheless, not My will, but Yours, be done," we see outlined the prayer of consecration and dedication. He was praying, in effect, "If there is any other way to do this, let's do it that way." But the key for Jesus, and for us, is, "Nevertheless not My will, but Yours, be done."

You pray that God's will would be done when you don't know His will or don't know if an alternative path that appears is equally "correct" or godly. In the absence of direct instructions, the prayer of consecration and dedication says you will allow God to set your direction or make your decisions.

The prayer of consecration and dedication works when you have two (or more) godly alternatives before you, and you are not getting a clear sense at that time about which option God wants you to take. When the direction is unclear but any of the options appear to be legitimate, righteous options, that is the perfect time to say, "Lord, if it be Your will."

Believe me, He will let you know if you are taking the wrong fork in the road.

The Prayer of Praise and Worship

In this prayer, you are not asking God to do something for you or to give you something. You are not even asking for direction and dedicating your life to whatever it is God has called you to do. Rather, you just want to praise the Lord, to thank Him for His many blessings and mercy. You want to tell Him how much you love Him.

A good example of this type of prayer appears in Luke 2:20, which describes the reaction of the shepherds who had seen baby Jesus.

In Luke 18:43, the blind man who was healed was described as "glorifying God." The verse also says all the people who witnessed the miracle "gave praise to God." They prayed prayers of thanksgiving.

Look at the way Jesus prayed in John 11:41: "Father, I *thank You* that You have heard Me," referring to His previous prayer regarding Lazarus.

Paul wrote to the Philippians that even when we pray the prayer of faith, we should always intersperse worship and praise.

> *Be anxious for nothing, but in everything by prayer and supplication, with thanksgiving, let your requests be made known to God (Phil. 4:6 KJV).*

The Prayer of Intercession

Intercession means you are interceding or acting in prayer on behalf of someone else. The person may be incapable of praying for himself. Perhaps he is on drugs or mentally confused by demonic doctrines. Perhaps the person is so sick he can't muster the energy to stay awake, let alone pray.

Intercession involves praying for others. It may involve praying in a general way for such things as the church or the government, or offering up more specific prayers based on your knowledge of a person's need.

Therefore I also, after I heard of your faith in the Lord Jesus and your love for all the saints, do not cease to give thanks for you, making mention of you in my prayers; that the God of our Lord Jesus Christ, the Father of glory, may give to you the spirit of wisdom and revelation in the knowledge of Him, the eyes of your understanding being enlightened; that you may know what is the hope of His calling, what are the riches of the glory of His inheritance in the saints. (Eph. 1:15–18 KJV)

Here Paul makes it plain that he prayed regularly for the church at Ephesus and for the individuals there to receive these blessings. He does not set himself in agreement with anyone, so this seems to be a good example of intercessory prayer.

The Prayer of Binding and Loosing

This prayer is found in Matthew.

Jesus says: "Assuredly, I say to you, whatever you bind on earth will be bound in heaven, and whatever you loose on earth will be loosed in heaven. Again, I say to you that if two of you agree on earth concerning anything that they ask, it will be done for them by My Father in heaven." (Matt. 18:18–19 KJV)

There are several important nuggets in Jesus's statements here, the first being that we have authority here on this earth by virtue of our covenant rights through Jesus. The second thing we notice is the direction of the action. Things do not begin in heaven and come to earth, but rather the action starts here on earth. Notice that it says, "Whatever you bind on earth will be bound in heaven, and whatever you loose on earth will be loosed in heaven."

Like all things in God's system, this type of prayer works only in line with God's Word and His laws. You cannot bind things willy-nilly. Binding a team to lose in the Super Bowl won't work any more than loosing someone to love you.

You can, however, bind foul spirits that are at work in people's lives or loose angelic spirits to work on your behalf in those areas where God has already promised you results. When you pray in this manner, God affirms it in heaven and puts His seal of approval on your prayer. Binding and loosing have to be based on the authority God has granted you in Scripture, not on some desire you have.

God has provided each type of prayer for a specific purpose. Though you may use more than one at any given time, it is important to be clear about which type you are using and why, and to be aware of its limitations. If you follow the examples in the Bible, you'll be sure to use them properly.

The Bible reveals many types of prayers and employs a variety of words to describe the practice. For example, 1 Timothy 2:1 (KJV) says, "First of all, then, I urge that supplications, prayers, intercessions, and thanksgivings be made for all people." Here, all four of the main Greek words used for prayer are mentioned in one verse.

In "The Celebration of the Christian Mystery," St. Thomas Aquinas, in the *Summa Theologica*, describes similar types of prayers in the Bible as follows.

The Prayer of Faith

> *And the prayer of faith will save the one*
> *who is sick, and the Lord will raise him up.*
> *(James 5:15 KJV)*

In this context, prayer is offered in faith for someone who is sick, asking God to heal. When we pray, we are to believe in the power and goodness of God (Mark 9:23).

We don't have to inform God of the problem or try to justify why He should grant our request but always give thanks for the solution. Jesus is the solution.

The Prayer of Agreement (Also Known as Corporate Prayer)

After Jesus's ascension, the disciples "all joined together constantly in prayer" (Acts 1:14 KJV). Later, after Pentecost, the early church "devoted themselves" to prayer (Acts 2:42 KJV). Their example encourages us to pray with others.

The Prayer of Request (Or Supplication)

We are to take our requests to God. Philippians 4:6 teaches, "Do not be anxious about anything, but in everything by prayer and supplication with thanksgiving let your requests be made known to God." Part of winning the spiritual battle is to be "praying at all times in the Spirit, with all prayer and supplication" (Eph. 6:18 KJV).

The Prayer of Thanksgiving

We see another type of prayer in Philippians 4:5 (KJV): "With thanksgiving let your requests be made known to

God." Many examples of thanksgiving prayers can be found in the Psalms.

The Prayer of Worship

The prayer of worship is similar to the prayer of thanksgiving. The difference is that worship focuses on who God is; thanksgiving focuses on what God has done. Church leaders in Antioch prayed in this manner with fasting: "While they were worshiping the Lord and fasting, the Holy Spirit said, 'Set apart for me Barnabas and Saul for the work to which I have called them.' Then after fasting and praying they laid their hands on them and sent them off" (Acts 13:2–3 KJV).

The Prayer of Imprecation

Imprecatory prayers are found in the Psalms (e.g., 7, 55, 69). They are used to invoke God's judgment on the wicked and thereby avenge the righteous. The psalmists use this type of appeal to emphasize the holiness of God and the surety of His judgment. Jesus teaches us to pray for blessing on our enemies, not cursing (Matt. 5:44–48).

The Bible also speaks of praying in the Spirit (1 Cor. 14:14–15 KJV) and prayers when we are unable to think of adequate words (Rom. 8:26–27 KJV). In those times, the Spirit Himself makes intercession for us.

Prayer is conversation with God and should be made without ceasing (1 Thess. 5:16–18). As we grow in our love for Jesus Christ, we will naturally desire to talk to Him. ("The Celebration of the Christian Mystery," St. Thomas Aquinas, in *Summa Theologica*).

Faith: We Are to Access God's Grace Through Faith

What Is Faith?

Faith can be compared to money. We use money in the world to buy things that we need or desire in the world. Faith functions the same way in the spiritual realm, where we can procure spiritual and physical needs and desires. God made mankind with a physical body with needs and a spiritual body with needs, and as Christians, we live in both realms.

> *Now faith is the substance of things hoped for, the evidence of things not seen. (Heb. 11:1 KJV)*

God, in the beginning, created heaven and earth. He did this by speaking creative words, like, "Let there be light," and there was light. Our words may be creative like God's Word if we believe (have faith) that all things are possible through Jesus; we have authority by aligning our words with what God says in His Written Word and, by faith, operate in the invisible realm, calling those things that are not as though they were (Rom. 4:17, Rom. 10:8–9). Faith is not just mental assent but is an action that has a destination or goal and operates in the present. Faith is believing and trusting what God says is true. Faith in the future tense is really hope and not faith at all. Hope may be the starting point for faith. Hope is a good thing, but it is not faith. Hope and imagination are related and have nearly the same definition. Both hope and imagination can be used for good or for evil.

Imagination

There is a mystery about mankind's ability to imagine things. In Genesis 6:5, God says that there is no hope for mankind because of their evil imaginations continually. These evil imaginations caused God to destroy life on earth by the flood. Only Noah and his family were saved. Apparently, mankind has a choice to imagine good or evil. Imagining something, coupled with faith, may have some creative force to bring it to reality.

> *The LORD saw that the wickedness (depravity) of man was great on the earth, and that every imagination or intent of the thoughts of his heart were only evil continually. (Gen. 6:5 KJV)*

> *Finally, believers, whatever is true, whatever is honorable and worthy of respect, whatever is right and confirmed by God's word, whatever is pure and wholesome, whatever is lovely and brings peace, whatever is admirable and of good repute; if there is any excellence, if there is anything worthy of praise, think continually on these things [center your mind on them, and implant them in your heart]. (Phil. 4:8 KJV)*

> *Therefore I tell you, stop being worried or anxious (perpetually uneasy, distracted) about your life, as to what you will eat or what you will drink; nor about your body,*

> *as to what you will wear. Is life not more*
> *than food, and the body more than cloth-*
> *ing? Look at the birds of the air; they nei-*
> *ther sow [seed] nor reap [the harvest] nor*
> *gather [the crops] into barns, and yet your*
> *heavenly Father keeps feeding them. Are*
> *you not worth much more than they? And*
> *who of you by worrying can add one hour to*
> *[the length of] his life? (Matt. 6:25 AMP)*

Imagination is from the heart and is linked to hope in both the Hebrew and Greek languages.

In Hebrew, imagination is yay'-tser, from *Strong's Concordance* H3335; a form; figuratively, conception (i.e. purpose): frame, thing framed, imagination, mind, work. In the Greek imagination is: dee-an'-oy-ah; from *Strong's Concordance* G1223 and G3563; deep thought, properly, the faculty (mind or its disposition), by implication—imagination, mind, understanding.

And Hope is yaw-chal'; a primitive root; to wait; by implication, to be patient, hope—(cause to, have, make to) hope, be pained, stay, tarry, trust, wait.

Faith is that which goes ahead right now and holds onto what I desire until I can get there to receive it. It is believing what God says over circumstance. God calls himself the great "I Am," giving us a hint of this mystery of the present. Man has control of the "now" only and no control of the past or the future. God was teaching Israel about acting in faith at the battle of Jericho, where they acted on His word, marching around the city once every day, then seven times on the seventh day and shouting. Their action was marching and shouting; their goal was to take the city by eliminating the walls. God often said to them, "I give you the promised land [or city]. Now go and possess it." He says the same thing to us today through the New Testament: "By His stripes you are healed." Now go and possess this healing (or provision).

> *The word is near you, on your lips and in your heart (that is, the word of faith that we proclaim); because if you confess with your lips that Jesus is Lord and believe in your heart that God raised him from the dead, you will be saved. For one believes with the heart and so is justified, and one confesses with the mouth and so is saved. (Rom. 10:8–10 AMP)*

> *For verily I say unto you, That whosoever shall say unto this mountain, Be thou removed, and be thou cast into the sea; and shall not doubt in his heart, but shall believe that those things which he saith shall come to pass; he shall have whatsoever he saith. Therefore I say unto you, What things soever ye desire, when ye pray, believe that you receive them, and you shall have them. (Mark 11:23—24 KJV)*

> *Jesus answered and said unto them, Verily I say unto you, If ye have faith, and doubt not, ye shall not only do this which is done to the fig tree, but also if ye shall say unto this mountain, Be thou removed, and be thou cast into the sea; it shall be done. And all things, whatsoever ye shall ask in prayer, believing, ye shall receive. (Matt. 21:21–22 KJV)*

And this is the confidence that we have in him, that, if we ask any thing according to his will, he heareth us: And if we know that he hear us, whatsoever we ask, we know that we have the petitions that we desired of him. (1 John 5:14–15 KJV)

God says He gives a portion or measure of faith to everyone.

For I say, through the grace given unto me, to every man that is among you, not to think of himself more highly than he ought to think; but to think soberly, according as God hath dealt to every man the measure of faith. (Rom. 12:3 KJV)

How to build faith?

First, we fill ourselves with God's Word. We prepare our hearts by aligning ourselves with God's promises, and then we speak them back to God in faith-filled words. We ask, not beg or bargain, for what we desire, and it shall be provided. We are told to "stand and continue to stand in our beliefs." We are a spirit that speaks our words by declaring what we believe.

Consequently, faith comes from hearing the message, and the message is heard through the words of Christ. (Rom. 10:17 NKJV)

But just as we have the same spirit of faith that is in accordance with scripture—"I

*believed, and so I spoke"—we also believe,
and so we speak. (2 Cor. 4:13 NASB)*

Jesus's examples of faith. Jesus pointed out many aspects of faith and demonstrated how faith works in the New Testament gospels. In Mark 4:37–40, Jesus said the fearful have no faith. Fear may be the opposite of faith. In Matthew 6:30 and 14:25–31, Jesus said the doubtful have little faith. In Matthew 8:5–10, Jesus said a centurion had great faith who demonstrated humility and trust. Romans 4:20 and Galatians 2:20 talk about perfect faith that staggers not at adversity but praises God for all things.

> *And there arose a great storm of wind, and the waves beat into the ship, so that it was now full. And he was in the hinder part of the ship, asleep on a pillow: and they awake him, and say unto him, Master, carest thou not that we perish? And he arose, and rebuked the wind, and said unto the sea, Peace, be still. And the wind ceased, and there was a great calm. And he said unto them, why are ye so fearful? how is it that ye have no faith? (Mark 4:37–40 KJV)*

> *Wherefore, if God so clothe the grass of the field, which today is, and tomorrow is cast into the oven, shall he not much more clothe you, O ye of little faith? (Matt. 6:30 KJV)*

> *And in the fourth watch of the night Jesus went unto them, walking on the sea. And when the disciples saw him walking on the*

sea, they were troubled, saying, "It is a spirit"; and they cried out for fear. But straightway Jesus spake unto them, saying, Be of good cheer; it is I; be not afraid. And Peter answered him and said, Lord, if it be thou, bid me come unto thee on the water. And he said, Come. And when Peter was come down out of the ship, he walked on the water, to go to Jesus. But when he saw the wind boisterous, he was afraid; and beginning to sink, he cried, saying, Lord, save me. And immediately Jesus stretched forth his hand, and caught him, and said unto him, O thou of little faith, wherefore didst thou doubt? (Matt. 14:25–31 KJV)

And when Jesus was entered into Capernaum, there came unto him a centurion, beseeching him, And saying, Lord, my servant lieth at home sick of the palsy, grievously tormented. And Jesus saith unto him, I will come and heal him. The centurion answered and said, Lord, I am not worthy that thou shouldest come under my roof: but speak the word only, and my servant shall be healed. For I am a man under authority, having soldiers under me: and I say to this man, Go, and he goeth; and to another, Come, and he cometh; and to my servant, Do this, and he doeth it. When Jesus heard it, he marvelled, and said to them that followed, Verily I say unto you, I

*have not found so great faith, no, not in
Israel. (Matt. 8:5–10 KJV)*

*He staggered not at the promise of God
through unbelief; but was strong in faith,
giving glory to God. (Rom. 4:20 KJV)*

*I am crucified with Christ: nevertheless, I
live; yet not I, but Christ liveth in me: and
the life which I now live in the flesh I live
by the faith of the Son of God, who loved
me, and gave himself for me. (Gal. 2:20
KJV)*

*And when they could not come nigh unto
him for the press, they uncovered the roof
where he was: and when they had broken it
up, they let down the bed wherein the sick
of the palsy lay. When Jesus saw their faith,
he said unto the sick of the palsy, Son, thy
sins be forgiven thee. (Mark 2:4 KJV)*

When the lame man was lowered down through the
roof, Jesus declared their faith had allowed the healing. The
lame man, too, demonstrated faith when he tried to get to his
feet when commanded to arise and walk.

Now, how do we live by faith?

In a broad sense, salvation covers all our needs in every
part of our lives—spiritual, emotional, social, mental, physical, financial, and material. Salvation is a free gift from God
and is received not by knowing about God's promise but
accepting and acting upon the promises. Salvation usually
starts with a desire to get right with God. God supplies faith

to believe that He is real, and He rewards those that diligently seek Him. Faith is something we are doing or saying, not something we have. Faith is acting on God's Word. Faith is acting like God's Word is true. Faith is trusting God. Our words reflect our faith; they line up with God's Word. Speaking words is required to walk in faith. We have access to the grace of God through speaking, declaring, and decreeing. We confess our faith in Jesus with our mouth for salvation. To confess is to speak out what we believe. We confess Jesus as our Lord and Savior, our provider, our righteousness, our healer, our strength.

> *The word is nigh thee, even in thy mouth, and in thy heart: that is, the word of faith, which we preach; That if thou shalt confess with thy mouth the Lord Jesus, and shalt believe in thine heart that God hath raised him from the dead, thou shalt be saved. For with the heart man believeth unto righteousness; and with the mouth confession is made unto salvation. (Rom. 10:8 KJV)*

> *Whosoever therefore shall confess me before men, him will I confess also before my Father which is in heaven. But whosoever shall deny me before men, him will I also deny before my Father which is in heaven. (Matt. 10:32 KJV)*

Faith requires action. To be obedient to God's Word, we are water-baptized, submersing underwater, which represents being buried by faith with Christ and raised a new person. We learn how to be humble and how to repent daily. We learn about the promise of the Holy Spirit and are led to receive Him into our hearts by faith (Acts 2:4). We become the temples of the living God. Our hearts are renewed; we are born again and start to see the kingdom of God (John 3:2–7, Titus 3:5). And we learn to act on the authority given us by Jesus (Mark 16:17). We are given spiritual gifts to help others and ourselves (1 Cor. 12:8–10). We learn how to praise and worship in spirit and truth. Submission costs something. Probably your most-prized possession. God wants to be first in our life. He wants us to depend on Him and not on magic, worldly knowledge, or anything else. He deserves to be first in our lives.

Jesus taught that words come from our spirit or heart and can defile us or bring blessing.

In other words, you get what you speak.

> *That if thou shalt confess with thy mouth the Lord Jesus, and shalt believe in thine heart that God hath raised him from the dead, thou shalt be saved. For with the heart man believeth unto righteousness; and with the mouth confession is made unto salvation. (Rom. 10:9–10 KJV)*

We need faith to please God and receive from Him the salvation He wants us to have.

> *But without faith it is impossible to please him (God): for he that cometh to God must believe that he is, and that he is a rewarder of them that diligently seek him. (Heb. 11:6 KJV)*

Salvation can be thought of as a walk with God through life. We start gaining wisdom, knowledge, and understanding through God's Word and circumstances of life. Now that we know how to ask in faith, the infinite God and His resources become available to us.

Therefore, being justified by faith, we have peace with God through our Lord Jesus Christ: By whom also we have access by faith into this grace wherein we stand, and rejoice in hope of the glory of God. (Rom. 5:1–2 KJV)

My son, attend to my words; incline thine ear unto my sayings. Let them not depart from thine eyes; keep them in the midst of thine heart. (Prov. 4:20–21 KJV)

For therein is the righteousness of God revealed from faith to faith: as it is written, "The just shall live by faith." (Rom. 1:17)

And this is the confidence that we have in him, that, if we ask any thing according to his will, he heareth us: And if we know that he hear us, whatsoever we ask, we know that we have the petitions that we desired of him. (1 John 5:14–15 KJV)

For we walk by faith, not by sight. (2 Cor. 5:7 KJV)

> *Thou art snared with the words of thy mouth, thou art taken with the words of thy mouth. (Prov. 6:2 KJV)*

> *Hast thou faith? have it to thyself before God. Happy is he that condemneth not himself in that thing which he alloweth. And he that doubteth is damned if he eat, because he eateth not of faith: for whatsoever is not of faith is sin. (Rom. 14:22 KJV)*

> *Jesus answered and said unto them, Verily I say unto you, If ye have faith, and doubt not, ye shall not only do this which is done to the fig tree, but also if ye shall say unto this mountain, Be thou removed, and be thou cast into the sea; it shall be done. And all things, whatsoever ye shall ask in prayer, believing, ye shall receive. (Matt. 21:21 KJV)*

We must understand who God is (He is good) and who we are in Christ (He has given us righteousness and authority).

Jesus said thus:

> *He that believeth and is baptized shall be saved; but he that believeth not shall be damned. And these signs shall follow them that believe; In my name shall they cast out devils; they shall speak with new tongues; They shall take up serpents; and if they drink any deadly thing, it shall not hurt*

them; they shall lay hands on the sick, and they shall recover. (Mark 16:16–18 KJV)

Verily, verily, I say unto you, He that believeth on me, the works that I do shall he do also; and greater works than these shall he do; because I go unto my Father. And whatsoever ye shall ask in my name, that will I do, that the Father may be glorified in the Son. If ye shall ask any thing in my name, I will do it. (John 14:12–14 KJV)

We are starting to understand how faith works through quantum physics.

Quantum Physics Defined

Quantum mechanics (QM, also known as quantum physics, or quantum theory) is a branch of physics that deals with physical phenomena at microscopic scales, where the action is on the order of the Planck constant. Quantum mechanics departs from classical mechanics primarily at the quantum realm of atomic and subatomic length scales. Quantum mechanics provides a mathematical description of much of the dual particle-like and wavelike behavior and interactions of energy and matter.

The name quantum mechanics derives from the observation that some physical quantities can change only in discrete amounts (Latin quanta) and not in a continuous (cf. analog) way. For example, the angular momentum of an electron bound to an atom or molecule is quantized. In the context of quantum mechanics, the wave-particle duality of energy and matter and the uncertainty principle provide a unified view of the behavior of photons, electrons, and other atomic-scale objects.

Note: In a 700 Club interview on November 7, 2019, Annette Capps revealed how faith may work in the quantum physics realm. Words are packets of faith that affect matter. God made us a speaking spirit (Rom. 12 TPT).

Quantum Faith

For verily I say unto you, That whosoever shall say unto this mountain, Be thou removed, and be thou cast into the sea; and shall not doubt in his heart, but shall believe that those things which he saith shall come to pass; he shall have whatsoever he saith. (Mark 11:23 KJV)

Then came the disciples to Jesus apart, and said, "Why could not we cast him out?" And Jesus said unto them, Because of your unbelief: for verily I say unto you, If ye have faith as a grain of mustard seed, ye shall say unto this mountain, Remove hence to yonder place; and it shall remove; and nothing shall be impossible unto you. (Matt. 17:19 KJV)

And when the disciples saw it, they marveled, saying, "How soon is the fig tree withered away!" Jesus answered and said unto them, Verily I say unto you, If ye have

*faith, and doubt not, ye shall not only do
this which is done to the fig tree, but also if
ye shall say unto this mountain, Be thou
removed, and be thou cast into the sea; it
shall be done. (Matt. 21:20–21 KJV)*

Looking at it from a surface level, it would seem a ridiculous statement that Jesus made. How is it possible that spoken words would send a mountain into the sea? For the past twenty-seven years, it has required faith on my part to believe that my words are powerful. Recent study in the area of quantum physics, however, has convinced me that what Jesus spoke is absolute scientific fact!

The disciples asked Jesus to increase their faith (Luke 17:5), and Jesus told them how in the next verse:

*And the apostles said unto the Lord, Increase
our faith.*

*And the Lord said, If ye had faith as a
grain of mustard seed, ye might say unto
this sycamine tree, Be thou plucked up by
the root, and be thou planted in the sea;
and it should obey you. (Luke 17:5–6 KJV)*

Mustard Seeds and Quantum Physics

When Jesus said, "If you have faith as a grain of mustard seed, you would say…," He was speaking of a very small seed common in His time. If He were here today, He might say, "If you had faith as an atom…," or, even smaller, "If you had faith as a quark [which is a subatomic particle]…" The point He was making was that small things that cannot be easily seen manifest themselves and affect things in this larger world where we live.

> *Through faith we understand that the worlds were framed by the word of God, so that things which are seen were not made of things which do appear. (Heb. 11:3 KJV)*

The chocolate cake you ate yesterday was made from things that do not appear. The recipe calls for water (H_2O). Before the hydrogen and oxygen combined into water, you could not see anything, yet the substance was there. Before God spoke and said, "Let there be light," the substance for light was there. The sound vibration of His words caused the substance to manifest and appear.

The Large Hadron Collider (LHC)

From Wikipedia

Many physicists hope that the Large Hadron Collider will help answer some of the fundamental open questions in physics, which concern the basic laws governing the interactions of forces among the elementary objects, the deep structure of space and time, and in particular, the interrelation between quantum mechanics and general relativity.

The term *hadron* refers to subatomic composite particles composed of quarks held together by the strong force (as atoms and molecules are held together by the electromagnetic force). The best-known hadrons are the baryons, such as protons and neutrons; hadrons also include mesons, such as the pion and kaon, which were discovered during cosmic ray experiments in the late 1940s and early 1950s.

A *collider* is a type of a particle accelerator with two directed beams of particles. In particle physics, colliders are used as a research tool: they accelerate particles to very high kinetic energies and let them impact other particles. Analysis of the by-products of these collisions gives scientists good evidence of the structure of the subatomic world and the laws of nature governing it. Many of these by-products are produced only by high-energy collisions, and they decay after very short periods. Thus, many of them are hard or nearly impossible to study in other ways. Scientists are exploring dark matter and other dimensions, as predicted by various models based on string theory. There is evidence of up to ten dimensions in our reality that may explain why God says that His ways are much higher than our ways and His thoughts are much higher than our thoughts. God is smart!

Words from Our Spirit Activate the Grace of God

Words are energy, and energy affects matter. The energy of your microwave vibrates the water molecules and heats the water. The energy of electricity flows to your washing machine and powers the motor that spins the tub and cleans your clothes. So we can rightfully say that energy affects matter. Jesus said that words are energy that affects the matter in your life. When you speak words like, "This is the worst car I have ever had, you stupid piece of junk!" those words are vibrations of energy that affect the atoms that make up that car. If you speak those words long enough, your car will obey you!

Scientists have performed experiments with atoms and their subatomic particles, such as electrons. If you paid attention in school, you saw the diagram of an atom with the electron orbiting it like the earth orbits the sun.

The interesting thing is that scientists have discovered that the electron that is shown orbiting the nucleus is not always there in particle form. It exists in a wave state (like a cloud, everywhere at once) until someone looks at it. When the scientist observes it, it suddenly appears as a dot (particle). What we all want to know is, how does it know someone is looking at it? It obviously is responding to the observer.

One of the difficulties in quantum physics is that the particles behave somewhat differently for each observer, which leads me to the question, does it behave according to what the scientist believes? In any event, we can definitely conclude that Jesus was right when He taught that all matter responds to faith and words. The substance from which our world is made is influenced and manifested by words. The things that you desire are made up of atoms. They know what you believe, hear what you say, and behave accordingly! "Say unto the mountain, 'Be removed,' and it will obey you."

Beliefs Produce Energy

Believing the thoughts and beliefs that you carry also produce an energy around you. Have you ever noticed that when you are angry, things go wrong and people are insulting and angry with you? Your thoughts and beliefs produce an energy that people can perceive and react to. If you believe that no one likes you, then you put off that rejecting type of energy, and people will be driven away from you.

If you love people and care about them, they will feel that and be drawn to you. Have you ever been around someone who is pleasant and full of love? It is an energy you can actually feel. The energy of love is a powerful drawing card for good in your life. After all, God is love.

When you believe that God loves you and wants you to prosper, then you change your words and beliefs about money. When financial challenges used to come my way, I would fall into fear and begin to say things like, "Well, now we won't be able to pay off the car, house, or whatever!" The fear and speaking of it is an energy that affects your checking account and stops financial freedom. Now, I have learned to think and believe and say, "Things always work out for me. Everything that I do prospers, and I have abundance in Jesus's name." God is not limited to the things that you and I see. There is an infinite supply of substance waiting to be manifest according to your beliefs and words!

Things Obey Words

Things obey words. Well, bringing things down to their atomic level and learning that scientifically these particles respond to people has had a significant effect on my faith. When Jesus spoke to the fig tree and said, "No man eat fruit from thee hereafter forever," then that fig tree dried up from the atomic level because of His words. When He spoke to the winds and the waves, they obeyed Him. He was teaching us the undeniable biblical principle that things obey faith-filled words.

Jesus did not demonstrate this just to prove He was the Son of God. He demonstrated it and then told His disciples that they, too, can speak words of power. He wanted us to have the revelation that we are powerful spirit beings who can speak to the mountains in our life and they will obey us. God already knows what we need before we ask and has already provided it.

One of the reasons that some people have a hard time believing this principle is that sometimes it takes a long time for things to manifest from the unseen into this seen realm. It especially takes a long time when you dig up your seed every day to see if anything is happening yet! The seed will produce in its time if you leave it alone. We are told to stand firm, continue to stand, and not waver in our faith.

Do you believe that the words you speak come to pass? From this time on, listen to what you are saying to the things around you. Are you speaking curses to your checkbook? Are you telling it to dry up from the roots? How about your children? What are you telling them? They will obey your prophecies of failure and delinquency and your blessings.

Things are responding to your words every day, so speak good things to all that surround your life. If you really believe Jesus's words, you will monitor your thoughts and conversations, because you are the one giving substance to your world through words! (See Annette Capps book 9780961897550, *Quantum Faith*.)

Service

God wants us to serve one another and spread the good news of the gospel. Jesus gave his disciples orders to go out and teach others about God and His plan of salvation (Matt. 28:16–20; John 20:21–23). He also said wait until you receive power from heaven, the comforter, the Holy Spirit, that will lead and guide you. Jesus said that when we help others, we are helping God. It is natural for us to use our carnal strength, experience, and understanding, but Jesus said we could do nothing without Him.

> *I am the Vine; you are the branches. The one who remains in Me and I in him bears much fruit, for [otherwise] apart from Me [that is, cut off from vital union with Me] you can do nothing. (John 15:5 KJV)*

It is an amazing satisfaction when doors open and opportunities arise suddenly and you have the perfect words to say to someone. Or you are led to someone who has just asked God for help and there you are with the solution to their need. When a person does more by accident without planning than others do through complicated programs, one knows they are partnered with God. God will not push anyone into service but waits for them to ask with their whole heart, believing that He can and will work with them. Service becomes fun and never stressful.

Lifestyle (2 Cor. 11:15; Rom. 12)

Pride is the number one obstacle that separates us from God. It is like a two-sided coin. One side is self-centeredness or selfishness, and the other side is shyness, worrying about what others think of us all the time. Both are over concern about self.

Romans chapter 12 serves as a good guideline for a good lifestyle.

I beseech you therefore, brethren, by the mercies of God, that ye present your bodies a living sacrifice, holy, acceptable unto God, which is your reasonable service. And be not conformed to this world: but be ye transformed by the renewing of your mind, that ye may prove what is that good, and acceptable, and perfect, will of God. For I say, through the grace given unto me, to every man that is among you, not to think of himself more highly than he ought to think; but to think soberly, according as God hath dealt to every man the measure of faith. For as we have many members in one body, and all members have not the same office: So we, being many, are one body in Christ, and every one members one of another. Having then gifts differing according to the grace that is given to us, whether prophecy, let us prophesy according to the proportion of faith; Or ministry, let us wait on our ministering: or he that teacheth, on teaching; Or he that exhorteth, on exhortation: he that giveth, let him do it with simplicity; he that ruleth, with diligence; he that sheweth mercy, with cheerfulness. Let love be without dissimulation. Abhor that which is evil; cleave to that which is good. Be kindly affectioned one to another with brotherly love; in honour preferring one another; Not slothful in business; fervent in spirit; serving the Lord; Rejoicing in hope; patient in tribulation; continuing instant in prayer; Distributing to the necessity of saints; given to hospitality. Bless them which persecute you: bless, and curse not. Rejoice with them that do rejoice, and weep with them that weep. Be of the same mind one toward another. Mind not high things, but condescend to men of low estate. Be not wise in your own conceits. Recompense to no man evil for evil. Provide things honest in the sight of all men. If it be possible, as much as lieth in you, live peaceably with all men. Dearly beloved, avenge not yourselves, but rather give place unto wrath: for it is written, Vengeance is mine; I will repay, saith the Lord. Therefore if thine enemy hunger, feed him; if he thirst, give him drink: for in so doing thou shalt heap coals of fire on his head. Be not overcome of evil, but overcome evil with good. (Rom. 12:1– 21 KJV)

Hearing the Voice of God

It is normal Christianity to hear directly from God, but we so often turn to other people, books, magazines, and denominational literature for advice. When we rely on our own experience to make decisions, we alienate God, who wants the best for us. His "proceeding" word is like signposts along our daily walk.

My sheep hear my voice, and I know them, and they follow me. (John 10:27 KJV)

But he answered and said, It is written, Man shall not live by bread alone, but by every word that proceedeth out of the mouth of God. (Duet. 8:3 KJV; Matt. 4:4 KJV)

Not everyone that saith unto me, Lord, Lord, shall enter into the kingdom of heaven; but he that doeth the will of my Father which is in heaven. Many will say to me in that day, Lord, Lord, have we not prophesied in thy name? and in thy name have cast out devils? and in thy name done many wonderful works? And then will I profess unto them, I never knew you: depart from me, ye that work iniquity. (Matt. 7:21–23 KJV)

Take my yoke upon you, and learn of me; for I am meek and lowly in heart: and ye shall find rest unto your souls. For my yoke is easy, and my burden is light. (Matt. 11:29–30 KJV)

Now we have received, not the spirit of the world, but the spirit which is of God; that we might know the things that are freely given to us of God. Which things also we speak, not in the words which man's wisdom teacheth, but which the Holy Ghost teacheth; comparing spiritual things with spiritual. (1 Cor. 2:12–13 KJV)

Where is the wise? where is the scribe? where is the disputer of this world? hath not God made foolish the wisdom of this world? But God hath chosen the foolish things of the world to confound the wise; and God hath chosen the weak things of the world to confound the things which are mighty. (1 Cor. 1:20 KJV)

When a believer is first born again (spiritual rebirth), our spirits are new, with no distractions or hindrances to hear God. But it is easy to slide back to worldly ways and become dull of hearing the Holy Spirit. We must avoid fear, unbelief, worry, discouragement, and distractions. And stay in thankfulness, worship, read our Bibles, pray, and talk to God throughout each day, stirring up the Holy Spirit within us.

The Spirit itself beareth witness with our spirit, that we are the children of God: And if children, then heirs; heirs of God, and joint-heirs with Christ; if so be that we suffer with him, that we may be also glorified together. (Rom. 8:16–17 KJV)

Of whom we have many things to say, and hard to be uttered, seeing ye are dull of hearing. (Heb. 5:11 KJV)

It is the spirit that quickeneth; the flesh profiteth nothing: the words that I speak unto you, they are spirit, and they are life. (John 6:63 KJV)

Martha was worried about many little things and was missing hearing God. (Luke 10:41 KJV)

Blessed are they which do hunger and thirst after righteousness: for they shall be filled. (Matt. 5:6 KJV)

This I say therefore, and testify in the Lord, that ye henceforth walk not as other Gentiles walk, in the vanity of their mind, Having the understanding darkened, being alienated from the life of God through the ignorance that is in them, because of the blindness of their heart. (Eph. 4:17 KJV)

But I fear, lest by any means, as the serpent beguiled Eve through his subtilty, so your minds should be corrupted from the simplicity that is in Christ. (2 Cor. 11:3 KJV)

That the God of our Lord Jesus Christ, the Father of glory, may give unto you the spirit of wisdom and revelation in the knowledge of him. (Eph. 1:17 KJV)

Understand that God is Spirit and communicates through a person's spirit often, bypassing their mind, even interrupting their thoughts. We are the temple of God, and the Holy Spirit dwells within us. Therefore, His voice is usually not audible (which would come from outside our temple). It requires faith to hear God; He communicates to each person as He desires, often in a small whisper, a nudge, a check in one's heart, a bump, a burning heart, a wind, feeling electricity, a prompting, or goose bumps, even pictures in our mind's eye. God often sends the same message several times through different people or media because we are so slow hearing His voice.

> *Know ye not that ye are the temple of God, and that the Spirit of God dwelleth in you? (1 Cor. 3:16 KJV)*

> *And what agreement hath the temple of God with idols? for ye are the temple of the living God; as God hath said, I will dwell in them, and walk in them; and I will be their God, and they shall be my people. (2 Cor. 6:16 KJV)*

> *He that believeth on me, as the scripture hath said, from within him shall flow rivers of living water. But this spake he of the Spirit, which they that believed on him were to receive: for the Spirit was not yet "given"; because Jesus was not yet glorified. (John 7:38–39 KJV)*

> *But I fear, lest by any means, as the serpent beguiled Eve in his craftiness, your minds should be corrupted from the simplicity and the purity that is toward Christ. (2 Cor. 11:3 KJV)*

> *The wind bloweth where it listeth, and thou hearest the sound thereof, but canst not*

> *tell whence it cometh, and whither it goeth:*
> *so is every one that is born of the Spirit.*
> *(John 3:8 KJV)*

Words of wisdom, words of knowledge, faith, and healing:

> *For to one is given by the Spirit the word of*
> *wisdom; to another the word of knowledge*
> *by the same Spirit; To another faith by the*
> *same Spirit; to another the gifts of healing*
> *by the same Spirit. (1 Cor. 12:8–9 KJV)*

Pictures, Visions, and Dreams

> *And it shall come to pass in the last days,*
> *saith God, I will pour out of my Spirit upon*
> *all flesh: and your sons and your daughters*
> *shall prophesy, and your young men shall see*
> *visions, and your old men shall dream*
> *dreams. (Acts 2:17 KJV)*

Expect to hear from God. Look up in anticipation to God, expecting an answer. Be prepared to write His answer down quickly before it is lost. Our minds have memory, but our spirit may quickly forget what God has spoken. If you find yourself rehearsing in your mind something over and over, then it probably did not come from God. If you hear the same message several times from different sources, it is usually from God. There are no coincidences.

*My voice shalt thou hear in the morning, O
LORD; in the morning will I direct my
prayer unto thee, and will look up. (Ps. 5:3
KJV)*

*And looking up to heaven, he sighed, and
saith unto him, Ephphatha, that is, be
opened. (Mark 7:34 KJV)*

*Then he took the five loaves and the two
fishes, and looking up to heaven, he blessed
them, and brake, and gave to the disciples
to set before the multitude. (Luke 9:16 KJV)*

Pray one thing at a time, listen for the answer, disarm
the enemy. Keep focused; avoid a wandering mind. Pray in
humility, with thanksgiving, worship, for we wrestle not
against flesh and blood.

*Humble yourselves in the sight of the Lord,
and he shall lift you up. (James 4:10 KJV)*

*For we wrestle not against flesh and blood,
but against principalities, against powers,
against the rulers of the darkness of this
world, against spiritual wickedness in high
places. (Eph. 6:12 KJV)*

Pray in the spirit, which is the perfect will of God. We
are made of body, soul, and spirit. We know the body has a
voice, and our mind (soul) has a voice (subconscious). May I

suggest our spirit (heart) also has a voice? Pray with your whole heart.

> *And he that searcheth the hearts knoweth what is the mind of the Spirit, because he maketh intercession for the saints according to the will of God. (Rom. 8:27 KJV)*

> *But ye, beloved, building up yourselves on your most holy faith, praying in the Holy Ghost. (Jude 1:20 KJV)*

> *Howbeit when he, the Spirit of truth, is come, he will guide you into all truth: for he shall not speak of himself; but whatsoever he shall hear, that shall he speak: and he will shew you things to come. (John 16:13 KJV)*

Pray fervently with the whole heart (wholeheartedly):

> *And he [Uzziah] sought God in the days of Zechariah, who had understanding in the visions of God: and as long as he sought the LORD, God made him to prosper. (2 Chron. 26:5 KJV)*

Sometimes we don't understand what he is saying. God's thoughts are higher than our thoughts. We must learn to see through His eyes.

> *Which things also we speak, not in the words which man's wisdom teacheth, but*

> *which the Holy Ghost teaches; comparing spiritual things with spiritual. (1 Cor. 2:13 KJV)*

Press on until breakthrough and peace are achieved. God likes persistence.

> *But without faith it is impossible to please him: for he that cometh to God must believe that he is, and that he is a rewarder of them that diligently seek him. (Heb. 11:6 KJV)*

God is all knowing and all powerful. God's word is already reality.

> *And Simon answering said unto him, Master, we have toiled all the night, and have taken nothing: nevertheless, at thy word I will let down the net. (Luke 5:5 KJV)*

> *Forever, O LORD, thy word is settled in heaven. (Ps. 119:89 KJV)*

Faith is seeing the unseen.

> *And the LORD said unto Joshua, See, I have given into thine hand Jericho, and the king thereof, and the mighty men of valor. (Josh. 6:2 KJV)*

> *And there sat a certain man at Lystra, impotent in his feet, being a cripple from his mother's womb, who never had walked:*

The same heard Paul speak: who steadfastly beholding him, and perceiving that he had faith to be healed, Said with a loud voice, Stand upright on thy feet. And he leaped and walked. (Acts 14:8–10 KJV)

Conclusion

In this chapter we have examined how we are to function while here on earth. We see that God is Spirit, and we have to relate to Him in spirit and truth. We have looked at some of the provisions God has given us to help us stay on track—the church, the sacraments, worship, prayer, faith, language, service, and lifestyle. We must hear from God before we can know the truth of a matter and get direction. We are trained to look at circumstances or experience in determining the truth, but Jesus wants us to hear His voice.

Jesus said, when He draws us, we seek Him. "No one can come to me unless the Father draws them" (John 6:44). Only the Holy Spirit can reveal the truth in Christ (John 15:26, 16:13; Matt. 16:16). When we seek Him with our whole heart, we find Him (Matt. 7:7; Luke 11:9). When we find Him, He invites us to join Him in His work. We get to know God through this process of sanctification. We carry His Word within us, but He does all the work and gets all the credit (Luke 17:21).

I have found that the best way to hear the voice of God is to pick up a pencil and paper. While you pray or meditate on Bible scriptures, write down the thoughts that pop up in your heart or mind and soon you will understand what God is saying to you.

In the last chapter, we will look at prophecy of end-time events and see what God's future plans may be. We have many good things ahead to look forward toward.

> *But as it is written, Eye hath not seen, nor ear heard, neither have entered into the heart of man, the things which God hath prepared for them that love him. (1 Cor. 2:9 KJV)*

CHAPTER 6

The Prophecy of Jesus Christ: End-Time Prophecy

Prophecy Overview

One-third of the Bible contains prophecy. It often reveals a shadow of future events for the purpose of showing mankind God's plans before they happen and, by this, reveals the omnipotent God, who has control over time and space. Prophecy is the reaction of an event like ripples are a reaction to a stone tossed in a pond. The ripples of prophecy often repeat over and over, like the ripples on the pond. The Word of God is so powerful that it can also cause the ripples to go in reverse back through time, like a play that is practiced over and over before the grand opening event. It also validates the scriptures, that they are from God. Most prophecy revolves around Israel and the world's Savior, Jesus Christ. The spirit of prophecy is the revelation of Jesus Christ.

Before we look at end-time prophecy, we should look at the prophecies that have already come to pass about Jesus. It is amazing to see the detail and accuracy of past predictions. There are over 330 fulfilled prophecies about Jesus and His first advent found in the Old Testament that have already come true. The books of Psalms and Isaiah contain the most. Here are just a few predictions from the book of Isaiah.

	Scripture	Prediction	Fulfillment
1.	Isaiah 2:3	He shall teach all nations.	John 4:25
2.	Isaiah 2:4	He shall judge among the nations.	John 5:22
3.	Isaiah 6:1	When Isaiah saw His glory.	John 12:40–41
4.	Isaiah 6:8	The One Sent by God.	John 12:38–45
5.	Isaiah 6:9–10	Parables fall on deaf ears.	Matthew 13:13–15
6.	Isaiah 6:9–12	Blinded to Christ and deaf to His words.	Acts 28:23–29
7.	Isaiah 7:14	To be born of a virgin.	Luke 1:35
8.	Isaiah 7:14	To be Emmanuel— God with us.	Matthew 1:18–23, 1 Timothy 3:16
9.	Isaiah 8:8	Called Emmanuel.	Matthew 28:20
10.	Isaiah 8:14	A stone of stumbling, a rock of offense.	1 Peter 2:8
11.	Isaiah 9:1–2	His ministry to begin in Galilee.	Matthew 4:12–17
12.	Isaiah 9:6	A child born—humanity.	Luke 1:31
13.	Isaiah 9:6	A Son given—deity.	Luke 1:32, John 1:14, 1 Timothy 3:16

14.	Isaiah 9:6	Declared to be the Son of God with power.	Romans 1:3, 4
15.	Isaiah 9:6	The Wonderful One, Peleh.	Luke 4:22
16.	Isaiah 9:6	The Counsellor, Yaatz.	Matthew 13:54
17.	Isaiah 9:6	The Mighty God, El Gibor.	1 Corinthians 1:24, Titus 2:13
18.	Isaiah 9:6	The Everlasting Father, Avi Adth.	John 8:58, 10:30
19.	Isaiah 9:6	The Prince of Peace, Sar Shalom.	John 16:33
20.	Isaiah 9:7	Inherits the throne of David.	Luke 1:32
21.	Isaiah 9:7	His character—just.	John 5:30
22.	Isaiah 9:7	No end to his government.	Luke 1:33
23.	Isaiah 11:1	Called a Nazarene-the Branch, Netzer.	Matthew 2:23
24.	Isaiah 11:1	A rod out of Jesse—Son of Jesse.	Luke 3:23, 32
25.	Isaiah 11:2	Anointed One by the Spirit.	Matthew 3:16, 17; Acts 10:38
26.	Isaiah 11:2	His character—wisdom, knowledge.	Colossians 2:3
27.	Isaiah 11:3	He would know their thoughts.	Luke 6:8, John 2:25
28.	Isaiah 11:4	Judge in righteousness.	Acts 17:31
29.	Isaiah 11:4	Judges with the sword of His mouth.	Revelations 2:16, 19:11, 19:15

30.	Isaiah 11:5	Character: Righteous and Faithful.	Revelations 2:16 19:11
31.	Isaiah 11:10	The Gentiles seek Him.	John 12:18–21
32.	Isaiah 12:2	Called Jesus-Yeshua.	Matthew 1:21
33.	Isaiah 22:22	The One given all authority to govern.	Revelation 3:7
34.	Isaiah 25:8	The Resurrection predicted.	1 Corinthians 15:54
35.	Isaiah 26:19	His power of Resurrection predicted.	Matthew 27:50–54
36.	Isaiah 28:16	The Messiah is the precious cornerstone.	Acts 4:11–12
37.	Isaiah 28:16	The Sure Foundation.	1 Corinthians 3:11, Matthew 16:18
38.	Isaiah 29:13	He indicated obedience to His Word.	Matthew 15:7–9
39.	Isaiah 29:14	The wise are confounded by the Word.	1 Corinthians 1:18–31
40.	Isaiah 32:2	A Refuge—a man shall be a hiding place.	Matthew 23:37
41.	Isaiah 35:4	He will come and save you.	Matthew 1:21
42.	Isaiah 35:5–6	To have a ministry of miracles.	Matthew 11:2–6
43.	Isaiah 40:3–4	Preceded by forerunner.	John 1:23

44.	Isaiah 40:9	"Behold your God."	John 1:36, 19:14
45.	Isaiah 40:10	He will come to reward.	Revelation 22:12
46.	Isaiah 40:11	A shepherd—compassionate life-giver.	John 10:10–18
47.	Isaiah 42:1–4	The Servant—as a faithful, patient redeemer.	Matthew 12:18–21
48.	Isaiah 42:2	Meek and lowly.	Matthew 11:28–30
49.	Isaiah 42:3	He brings hope for the hopeless.	Matthew 12:14–21; John 4:1–54
50.	Isaiah 42:4	The nations shall wait on His teachings.	John 12:20–26
51.	Isaiah 42:6	The Light (salvation) of the Gentiles.	Luke 2:32
52.	Isaiah 42:1, 6	His is a worldwide compassion.	Matthew 28:19–20
53.	Isaiah 42:7	Blind eyes opened.	John 9:25–38
54.	Isaiah 43:11	He is the only Savior.	Acts 4:12
55.	Isaiah 44:3	He will send the Spirit of God.	John 16:7, 13
56.	Isaiah 45:21–25	He is Lord and Savior.	Philippians 3:20, Titus 2:13
57.	Isaiah 45:23	He will be the Judge.	John 5:22; Romans 14:11
58.	Isaiah 46:9	Declares things not yet done.	John 13:19
59.	Isaiah 48:12	The First and the Last.	John 1:30; Revelation 1:8, 17

60.	Isaiah 48:16	He came as a Teacher.	John 3:2
61.	Isaiah 49:1	Called from the womb—His humanity.	Matthew 1:18
62.	Isaiah 49:5	A Servant from the womb.	Luke 1:31; Philippians 2:7
63.	Isaiah 49:6	He will restore Israel.	Acts 3:19–21, 15:16–17
64.	Isaiah 49:6	He is Salvation for Israel.	Luke 2:29–32
65.	Isaiah 49:6	He is the Light of the Gentiles.	John 8:12, Acts 13:47
66.	Isaiah 49:6	He is Salvation unto the ends of the earth.	Acts 15:7–18
67.	Isaiah 49:7	He is despised of the nation.	John 1:11, 8:48–49, 19:14–15
68.	Isaiah 50:3	Heaven is clothed in black at His humiliation.	Luke 23:44–45
69.	Isaiah 50:4	He is a learned counselor for the weary.	Matthew 7:29, 11:28–29
70.	Isaiah 50:5	The Servant bound willingly to obedience.	Matthew 26:39
71.	Isaiah 50:6	"I gave my back to the smiters."	Matthew 27:26
72.	Isaiah 50:6	He was smitten on the cheeks.	Matthew 26:67
73.	Isaiah 50:6	He was spat upon.	Matthew 27:30

74.	Isaiah 52:7	Published good tidings upon mountains.	Matthew 5:12, 15:29, 28:16
75.	Isaiah 52:13	The Servant exalted.	Acts 1:8–11; Ephesians 1:19–22; Philippians 2:5
76.	Isaiah 52:14	The Servant shockingly abused.	Luke 18:31–34; Matthew 26:67–68
77.	Isaiah 52:15	Nations startled by message of the Servant.	Luke 18:31–34; Matthew 26:67–68
78.	Isaiah 52:15	His blood shed sprinkles nations.	Hebrews 9:13–14, Revelation 1:5
79.	Isaiah 53:1	His people would not believe Him.	John 12:37–38
80.	Isaiah 53:2	Appearance of an ordinary man.	Philippians 2:6–8
81.	Isaiah 53:3	Despised.	Luke 4:28–29
82.	Isaiah 53:3	Rejected.	Matthew 27:21–23
83.	Isaiah 53:3	Great sorrow and grief.	Matthew 26:37–38, Luke 19:41
84.	Isaiah 53:3	Men hide from being associated with Him.	Mark 14:50–52
85.	Isaiah 53:4	He would have a healing ministry.	Matthew 8:16–17
86.	Isaiah 53:4	Thought to be cursed by God.	Matthew 26:66; 27:41–43
87.	Isaiah 53:5	Bears penalty for mankind's iniquities.	2 Corinthian 5:21; Hebrew 2:9

88.	Isaiah 53:5	His sacrifice provides peace between man and God.	Colossians 1:20
89.	Isaiah 53:5	His sacrifice would heal man of sin.	1 Peter 2:24
90.	Isaiah 53:6	He would be the sin-bearer for all mankind.	1 John 2:2; 4:10
91.	Isaiah 53:6	God's will that He bear sin for all mankind.	Galatians 1:4
92.	Isaiah 53:7	Oppressed and afflicted.	Matthew 27:27–31
93.	Isaiah 53:7	Silent before his accusers.	Matthew 27:12–14
94.	Isaiah 53:7	Sacrificial lamb.	John 1:29; 1 Peter 1:18–19
95.	Isaiah 53:8	Confined and persecuted.	Matthew 26:47–75; 27:1–31
96.	Isaiah 53:8	He would be judged.	John 18:13–22
97.	Isaiah 53:8	Killed.	Matthew 27:35
98.	Isaiah 53:8	Dies for the sins of the world.	1 John 2:2
99.	Isaiah 53:9	Buried in a rich man's grave.	Matthew 27:57
100.	Isaiah 53:9	Innocent and had done no violence.	Luke 23:41, John 18:38
101.	Isaiah 53:9	No deceit in his mouth.	1 Peter 2:22
102.	Isaiah 53:10	God's will that He die for mankind.	John 18:11

103. Isaiah 53:10	An offering for sin.	Matthew 20:28; Galatians 3:13
104. Isaiah 53:10	Resurrected and live forever.	Romans 6:9
105. Isaiah 53:10	He would prosper.	John 17:1–5
106. Isaiah 53:11	God fully satisfied with His suffering.	John 12:27
107. Isaiah 53:11	God's servant would justify man.	Romans 5:8–9, 18–19
108. Isaiah 53:11	The sin-bearer for all mankind.	Hebrews 9:28
109. Isaiah 53:12	Exalted by God because of his sacrifice.	Matthew 28:18
110. Isaiah 53:12	He would give up his life to save mankind.	Luke 23:46
111. Isaiah 53:12	Numbered with the transgressors.	Mark 15:27–28; Luke 22:37
112. Isaiah 53:12	Sin-bearer for all mankind.	1 Peter 2:24
113. Isaiah 53:12	Intercede to God on behalf of mankind.	Luke 23:34, Romans 8:34
114. Isaiah 55:3	Resurrected by God.	Acts 13:34
115. Isaiah 55:4	A witness.	John 18:37
116. Isaiah 55:4	He is a leader and commander.	Hebrews 2:10
117. Isaiah 55:5	God would glorify Him.	Acts 3:13
118. Isaiah 59:16	Intercessor between man and God.	Matthew 10:32
119. Isaiah 59:16b	He would come to provide salvation.	John 6:40

After the flood in 2349 BC, God set up the nations, as recorded in Genesis 9 and 10, and gave them each power to govern the earth as He desired, starting with the nations of the east, going westward, through time, to the United States. Each has failed in some way, but God's plan is to come with His kingdom and rule on earth as it is in heaven. Abraham was called by God about 1922 BC, and Moses about 1591 BC.

One of the prophetic ripples of Jesus coming to earth to save mankind may have been the dress rehearsal Passover, where God delivered His chosen people from Egyptian bondage. The details of the Passover story fit in many ways with the ministry of Christ. At Passover (May 5, 1491 BC, according to Roman history), when the Hebrews were delivered from Egyptian bondage, there were requirements for them to accomplish: (1) They had to believe that God was going to make the pharaoh let them go. (2) They had to follow Moses's directions of killing, roasting, and eating a lamb for each family and putting the blood on the doorposts of their houses for each family. (3) They had to eat the entire lamb and dress themselves for travel. This showed their faith, that they believed God and were leaving Egypt. Likewise, Christians must follow similar steps of believing God and the work of Christ. We prepare for heaven by increasing knowledge of God's kingdom. As an example, God fed them, clothed them, and taught them in the wilderness for forty years, and in similar fashion, we spend our lives being sanctified and learning about God's plans our whole life. Crossing over the Jordan River into the promised land is like mature Christians facing persecution once they are saved. Christians still have to fight just like Israel had to overcome the local inhabitants to take the promised land.

We have seen another ripple of prophecy in the book of Ruth that has an underlying prophecy of a Gentile bride being redeemed by a kinsman redeemer (Boaz), a type of Christ, and restoring Naomi (Israel) back to her land.

The book of Ester is a shadow of future end-time events, where Haman, symbolized as Satan, was destroyed along with his ten sons. In the books of Daniel and Revelation, the ten sons represent the ten toes or ten nations.

The books of Daniel and Revelation work together to reveal the end-time events leading up to the second coming of Christ and God's kingdom coming to earth. According to Revelation 1:19, the book of Revelation contains past, present, and future events leading up to the second return of Jesus Christ.

The following overview of the book of Revelation is how I currently believe events may unfold, but there is no private interpretation. Every generation has tried to fit these prophecies into their current generation. Only God knows the exact timing, but I believe we will know the season. Like God, the Bible is infinite in nature, and you may see other truths.

Chapters 1–3 describe the past and present events from God's point of view of seven major churches in Asia Minor. Starting with chapter 4, John observes future events from his time. The book of Revelation gives four separate accounts over different time intervals of the second return of Jesus Christ to earth. John tells these four stories of the future that all end at Christ's return at the battle of Armageddon. Chapters 4–8 give a coarse overview of events from about AD 325 to the battle of Armageddon in the form of seven seals. Chapters 8–11 of Revelation describe a more detailed account of events from about 1914 to Armageddon in the form of seven trumpets. Chapters 12–14 relate to the politi-

cal, religious, and economic plans of the one-world government and the two harvests of souls on the earth just before
Armageddon. The first harvest, represented by the wheat
harvest, may represent the rapture of the church. Chapters
15–19 give a detailed account of events starting from the
antichrist-controlled one-world government to the end of
the age, depicted by seven vials poured out onto the earth. All
four future accounts end at Armageddon and Christ's return
(see Rev. 8:5, Rev. 11:19, and Rev. 16:18 for story endings).
In Daniel 2, we see an overview of God's plans for the nations,
depicted by an image or statue. It is the story of God setting
up His kingdom on earth (Dan. 2:44). Babylon is depicted as
the head, Medes and Persia the arms and chest, Greece the
belly, Rome to possibly represent the legs (one leg the Holy
Roman Empire, the other the Byzantine Empire out of
Constantinople), and the feet with iron mixed with clay a
form of Roman government mixed with governments from
other nations (democracy and whatnot). Daniel chapter 7
and Revelation chapter 13 pick up where Daniel chapter 2
ends and tells the story in more detail of the nations near the
end of this age. The lion may be Great Britain, the bear
Russia, the leopard Germany that rises to power four times,
depicted by the four heads, and the United States is shown as
eagle's wings that came off Great Britain and stood as a man
(nation), so to speak. These prophecies were sealed up until
recently (Dan. 12:9) but are now being revealed to this
generation.

The book of Revelation is the dramatization of the
unveiling of Jesus Christ, past, present, and future. It records
the events of the church age and the second coming of our
Lord and Savior back to this earth. In verse 1 of chapter 4, we
move into the future, the prophetic part of the book of
Revelation from John's point of view. "After this I looked,

and, behold, a door was opened in heaven: and the first voice which I heard was as it were of a trumpet talking with me; which said, Come up hither, and I will shew thee things which must be hereafter."

Three Event Categories

The apostle John was inspired by God to write Revelation while he was exiled on the Isle of Patmos. It is not written in chronological order, but it is in an order, just not from front to back. I see three categories of the events in the book of Revelation according to Revelation 1:19—the things that John had already seen, the things "which are" (situations already existing in John's world), and future events, the things "which shall be hereafter." These future events are described in four short repeating stories that contain increasing detail: seven seals, seven trumpets, seven thunders, and seven vials.

Seven Seals

The seals are the long story (overview), ending with Armageddon and Jesus's return to earth at Revelation 8:5. The trumpets are the shorter story, with more detail, and ends at the same place, Christ's second coming at Revelation 11:19. The vials are the very short but detailed story, also ending at Armageddon, where Christ returns (Rev. 16:18). These stories, like the four gospels, tell the same story from four different perspectives. The sixth and seventh seal, the seventh trumpet, and the seventh vial all describe voices, lightning, thunders, an earthquake, and great hail. These all describe the same event, because they are the same event.

Each of them describes the second coming of Jesus Christ to this earth.

Sidenote Chapters

The skeletal structure of Revelation is contained in the seals, the trumpets, and the vials. Revelation also contains what some call detail chapters. They give us additional information not contained in the seals, trumpets, and vials. For example, Revelation chapter 12 describes a war that will take place in heaven three and one-half years before the second coming. Revelation chapter 13 foretells the coming one-world government, one-world religion, and the global economic system. Revelation chapters 17 and 18 contain a detailed account of the coming destruction of the false religious systems that will be in alliance with the antichrist.

Blessing and Curse

Revelation is the only book in the Bible that ends with a blessing on those who keep the sayings of the book, and a curse on those who add to or take away from the things written in the book.

> *Blessed is he that reads and they that hear the words of this prophecy, and keep those things which are written therein: for the time is at hand. (Rev. 1:3)*

> *If any man shall add unto these things, God shall add unto him the plagues that are*

written in this book: And if any man shall
take away from the words of the book of this
prophecy, God shall take away his part out
of the book of life, and out of the holy city,
and from the things which are written in
this book. (Rev. 22:18–19)

You and I may be part of the generation that will see the unveiling of Jesus Christ. The Bible has given us reliable signs that we are in the end-times. Jesus said, "So likewise ye, when ye shall see all these things, know that it is near, even at the doors. Verily I say unto you, this generation shall not pass, till all these things be fulfilled" (Matt. 24:33–34). Which generation will not pass until all these things are fulfilled? The answer is, the generation that shall see the things prophesied by Jesus in Matthew 24. I believe we are witnessing the fulfillment of these things right now!

Revelation 1

Revelation 1:7 reveals the entire theme of the book of Revelation, the coming of our Lord, Jesus Christ. "Behold, he cometh with clouds; and every eye shall see him."

Revelation 2–3

John opens with evaluation letters to the seven churches of Asia. Some theologians see characteristics of church types during the two-thousand-year church age.

The church at Ephesus were hardworking, suffering, and patient. Hated evil men and tested false apostles but had lost the love they first had.

The church at Smyrna had much trouble, was poor, and yet spiritually rich. Withstanding many satanic verbal attacks, testing, imprisonments, and even death. Stay faithful and you will not be hurt by the second death.

The church at Pergamum, where Satan lives, you have kept your faith even when Antipus was killed but have tolerated those who follow the teachings of Balaam, leading people to sin through sexual immorality and teachings of the Nicolaitans.

The church at Thyatira were faithful, loving, and served others, but you tolerate that woman Jezebel, who calls herself a messenger of God and is not. Who leads My people into sexual immorality and eating food that has been offered to idols. I have given her and her followers room to repent, and they will not. Unless they repent there will be terrible consequences. I know everyone's thoughts and deep secrets, and I will repay. Those of you that endure faithfully to the end will receive authority to rule the nations with an iron rod and receive the morning star.

The church at Sardis were dying spiritually but had a reputation of being a strong church. Jesus told them to wake up, repent, and revisit what they were taught or he would come like a thief at a time they are not expecting. Some in the church are faithful and will be clothed in white, and their names will not be removed from the Book of Life.

The church at Philadelphia followed Jesus's teachings and were faithful. They resisted the followers of Satan and endured, so Jesus was going to cause their enemies to bow down to this church and make known that God loves them. They will be safe in the time of trouble and will be a pillar in the temple of God. God will write on them the name of the city of New Jerusalem and the new name of Jesus.

The church at Laodicea was lukewarm, thinking they were rich but really poor spiritually. Jesus said he was going to spit them out of His mouth. He rebukes and punishes the ones He loves and asks them to repent and turn from their sins.

Revelation 4–5

We get a glimpse of heaven and see the worship of the one "who sits on the throne." The cry goes out, "Who is worthy to open the scroll and break its seven seals?" No one in all of heaven and earth was found worthy to open the scroll until the Lamb of God, Jesus Christ, stood in the midst of the throne.

Revelation 6

In chapter 6, the Lamb loosens the seals, revealing the four horsemen of the apocalypse, the souls under the altar, and the heavens departing like a scroll.

Revelation 7

Chapter 7 describes the sealing of the 144,000 to protect them from the calamities to come.

The later part of the chapter describes those that have come out of great tribulation. "These are they which came out of great tribulation, and have washed their robes, and made them white in the blood of the Lamb" (Rev. 7:14).

Revelation 8–11

Five of the first six trumpets reveal great catastrophes upon the nations, but the people still do not repent.

Every generation has tried to fit the predictions in Revelation into their history to understand where they are in the prophetic timetable. In this section we will examine recent historical events and try to fit them into the trumpet predictions. Jesus said we would not know the exact time, but we will know the season.

In 1914–1919, during World War I, a different type of battle emerged. Cannons were much larger, rockets flew back and forth like falling stars bursting with instant death, and a scorched-earth policy was put into effect because the battle lines moved back and forth so much that no one wanted to give their enemy anything green to eat or use. Machine guns mowed people down in great numbers, and the use of mustard gas killed as many friendly troops as the enemy. Instead of thousands dying, millions died—8.2 million to be exact. It was called the Great War. John might have seen this war in a vision and tried to record what he saw in Revelation 8:6.

In 1939–1946, during World War II, warfare again changed to the nuclear age. Resembling a mountain of fire enfolding itself near the edge of the sea, the two atomic bombs dropped on Japan brought death to millions of people. Large armies with large navies fought on land and sea. History shows 105,000 ships engaged in this war around the world, resulting in 36,000 being sunk. Almost exactly one-third. The death toll was fifty-two million people. You would expect such a horrific war would make its way into Bible prophecy. And maybe it did, as recorded by John in Revelation 8:8.

May 1948, the new Jewish nation was formed and Jews that were scattered all over the world started moving to Israel, as recorded in Ezekiel 20:34, Hosea 3:4–5, and Isaiah 11:11–12.

> *For the children of Israel shall abide many days without a king, and without a prince, and without a sacrifice, and without an image, and without an ephod, and without teraphim: Afterward shall the children of Israel return, and seek the Lord their God, and David their king; and shall fear the Lord and his goodness in the latter days. (Hosea 3:4–5 KJV)*

> *And it shall come to pass in that day, that the Lord shall set his hand again the second time to recover the remnant of his people, which shall be left, from Assyria, and from Egypt, and from Pathros, and from Cush, and from Elam, and from Shinar, and from Hamath, and from the islands of the sea. And he shall set up an ensign for the nations, and shall assemble the outcasts of Israel, and gather together the dispersed of Judah from the four corners of the earth. (Isa. 11:11–12 KJV)*

Not long after the Jews' arrival in Israel in 1948, the land started to bloom with fruits and flowers to the extent that it became Israel's main export to Europe. Since the Jews returned to this land, things have changed dramatically. One author in the 1800s counted the trees in Palestine and reported there were less than 1,000. Today there are more than 1.2 billion fully grown, mature trees. There was a conscious and concerted effort by the Jews to plant trees. Today, half of their trees are forest trees—half are fruit trees. Currently, Israel exports about 80 percent of its fruit harvest. As good as it is in the land today, during the millennium it will be increased dramatically.

> *I will open rivers in high places, and fountains in the midst of the valleys: I will make the wilderness a pool of water, and the dry land springs of water.*
>
> *I will plant in the wilderness the cedar, the shittah tree, and the myrtle, and the oil tree; I will set in the desert the fir tree, and the pine, and the box tree together:*
>
> *That they may see, and know, and consider, and understand together, that the hand of the Lord hath done this, and the Holy One of Israel hath created it. (Isa. 41:18–20 KJV)*

When people meditate on the Word of God and have a childlike belief that it is true, they often experience heavenly information downloaded to their heart.

> *But as it is written, Eye hath not seen, nor ear heard, neither have entered into the heart of man, the things which God hath prepared for them that love him. But God*

hath revealed them unto us by his Spirit: for the Spirit searcheth all things, yea, the deep things of God. For what man knoweth the things of a man, save the spirit of man which is in him? even so the things of God knoweth no man, but the Spirit of God. Now we have received, not the spirit of the world, but the spirit which is of God; that we might know the things that are freely given to us of God. Which things also we speak, not in the words which man's wisdom teacheth, but which the Holy Ghost teacheth; comparing spiritual things with spiritual. But the natural man receiveth not the things of the Spirit of God: for they are foolishness unto him: neither can he know them, because they are spiritually discerned. (1 Cor. 2:9–14 KJV)

April of 1986, another disaster struck in Pripyak (Prypyat), Russia, at the Chernobyl power plant when the number 4 nuclear reactor exploded, blew its top off, and shot bright, radioactive plasma over a mile into the sky. The radioactivity of this disaster was ten times that of the Japanese atomic bomb. The cesium 137 rained down on Europe for several months, poisoning the rivers and waterways of Europe from Sweden, Germany, England, and all the way to Italy. The disaster killed two million people immediately but may still be affecting the inhabitants of Europe with thyroid cancer and allergies to this day. Cesium 137 has a half-life of thirty years. What is very interesting is that in the English Bible, at Revelation 8:10–11, this mountain of fire that burns like a lamp is called Wormwood, which is *Chernobyl* in

Russian! Pick up any Russian Bible and read verse 11 and see if it doesn't say *Chernobyl* instead of *Wormwood!*

Jesus said in Matthew 24:32 that the days would be shortened during the end-times, and this may tie in with Revelation 8:12, where the sun did not shine for one-third of a day. Two events that occurred that ties in with the fourth trumpet may be the start of the new world order, and the Berlin Wall came down in 1989. Maybe God is accelerating events.

In August 1990 to February 1991 (just over five months), the Gulf War was waged against Iraq. There were seven hundred oil wells set on fire by Saddam Hussein as he was forced out of Kuwait. The heavy smoke turned day into night and blotted out the sky for three months as the world sent firefighters into the area to put out the intense fires. Thirty-four nations joined forces against Iraq in what was called Desert Shield and Desert Storm, which made quick work of all resistance. The many helicopters that came into Iraq, like a swarm of locust, brought troops and spread destruction on the aggressive nation. There were only 190 casualties reported for all the coalition countries, while Saddam's forces suffered about 26,000 casualties and 75,000 wounded. Many Iraqi soldiers fled in fear. There were not many friendly casualties for a war this size, just as recorded by John in Revelation 9:1–12. What is amazing is that the name of the Iraqi leader Saddam means "destroyer" in Arabic; Apollyon means "destroyer" in Greek, and Abaddon means "destroyer" in Hebrew, just like recorded in verse 11. In other words, the Bible names Saddam as the angel of the bottomless pit that ignited the fires and fought the world forces.

Between 2000 and 2010, earthquakes greater than 6 on the Richter scale increased 1,000 percent from previous decades. There was an average of 43 per decade of these size earthquakes in the world since 1900 until 2000, and from 2000 to 2010, there were 425. Jesus said in Matthew 24 that there would be an increase in earthquakes in the latter days. He was right again.

In 1999 and 2005, national ID card legislation was defeated in the US. A republic is formed to eliminate governmental control of the people, whereas a dictatorship wants to control the population. Of course, there are some advantages of convenience with a dictator, but the tradeoff is less freedom for everyone. In the future it is prophesied that a world leader will control the populace by controlling buying and selling (Rev. 13:17).

On November 29, 2012, the United Nations (UN) voted 128 to 9 to grant statehood to Palestine, allowing them to file charges against Israel in the International Criminal Courts. Since the 1967 war, Israel has occupied the Judea area of the West Bank and is considered now to be an aggressor. World sanctions have already been started banning Judean products from being bought or sold.

In 2015, the one-world government continued to form. Obama went to the UN instead of US Congress to get permission to make war on Libya. The Libyan Civil War was not approved by US Congress but by the UN, who used NATO world troops. This action was a big step toward globalization. We now are starting to hear terms such as "one-world bank," "one-world health care," and "one-world religion."

Revelation 9:13–21 describes a future war in the vicinity of the Euphrates River (Iraq, Syria, and Turkey) that has an army two million strong. Destruction comes from the mouth of a beast (bullets) and from the tail (bombs) mixed with brimstone, which may represent nuclear weapons. One-third of mankind is destroyed (Rev. 9:14–18). The whole region is presently at war (Ps. 83:1–18). Damascus is destroyed in one day (Isa. 17:1). And eyes and tongues within people disintegrate (Zech. 14:12).

A leader emerges on the scene, speaking great things and developing a peace treaty with Israel and Palestine for seven years (possibly a sharing arrangement of the Temple Mount in Jerusalem). In August 2020, a similar peace treaty was signed between Israel and UAE that may be the start of this covenant (Dan. 9:27). This may be the start of the seven-year tribulation period (Rev. 13:5–9; Dan. 12:11; Jer. 30:11; Matt 24).

The Jewish temple will soon be rebuilt in Jerusalem prior to the tribulation, and sacrifices will start again. (See Dan. 9:27 and 2 Thess. 2:3–4.)

About this time, we are told that Satan is thrown out of heaven to the earth and is full of anger because he knows his time is short. Three and a half years after the peace treaty is signed, the Jews on the West Bank will be slaughtered (Judea area) when the antichrist stands in the Jerusalem temple and declares himself God (abomination of desolation) (Matt. 24:15–22; 2 Thess. 2:3–4).

All nations gather against Israel except Jordan, and possibly the United States, who seem to resist the one-world government. The war of Gog and Magog may also be called Armageddon (Zech. 14:2; Ezek. 37–39).

And the rest of the men which were not killed by these plagues yet repented not of the works of their hands, that they should not worship devils, and idols of gold, and silver, and brass, and stone, and of wood: which neither can see, nor hear, nor walk: Neither repented they of their murders, nor

*of their sorceries, nor of their fornication,
nor of their thefts. (Rev. 9:20–21 KJV)*

God is maximizing the number of people that will be saved (2 Pet. 3:9). (*End Time Prophecy*, an Irwin Baxter TV program.)

Revelation 10

Then in Revelation 10:1–11, an angel gives John a scroll to eat that tastes sweet but is sour to the stomach. The sweetness may represent knowing the good things that God is going to do in the future, and the bitterness may represent the judgments yet to come. (See 1 Cor. 15:53; 1 Thess. 4:16–17; Rom. 8:11; Dan. 7:12.)

Revelation 11

The earthy temple is measured, and the outer court is set aside for the Gentiles. At the writing of this book, this temple is in the planning stages and has not been built yet.

Two witnesses with great power preach the gospel for 1,260 days and are then killed in Jerusalem. After three and a half days, God raises them back to life and brings them up to heaven in a cloud in front of everyone on earth.

Revelation 12

A woman with twelve stars about her head. The woman is depicted in the throes of childbirth. The dragon, Satan, stands before the woman to devour the child as soon as he is born. The woman is Israel, and the twelve stars symbolize the twelve tribes of Israel. The child is Jesus. Herod the Great did attempt to kill Jesus just as soon as He was born; however, he failed when Joseph took his family to Egypt.

The narrative of Revelation 12 appears to jump back two thousand years to when Jesus was born. Satan wages war against the forces of God in heaven but is defeated. Satan is cast out of heaven with his angels and confined to the earth. The dragon then wages war against Israel, but Israel is protected by the wings of a great eagle (USA). A beast rises from the sea, a confederation of world empires led by the antichrist. Another beast comes out of the earth, appearing as a lamb but speaking like the devil. This second beast, the false prophet, deceives the people of the earth, influencing them to worship the antichrist.

Revelation 13

This chapter describes the political (Rev. 13:1–10), the religious (Rev. 13:11–13), and the economic (Rev. 13:16–17) plans of this one-world government headed up by the antichrist. *Antichrist* does not mean "against Christ" but means "instead of Christ." The nations described in Daniel chapter 7 are again described in Revelation 13 with a little more detail. Germany depicted as a panther with four heads may represent the four times Germany will rise to power, and the fatal head wound may represent when the Third Reich Germany was cut in half from 1945 until 1989. Germany is on the rise again, and a book describing the Fourth Reich is already in bookstores today.

The mark of the beast is then implemented, maybe RFID chips for each person to control the economy, no buying or selling as the antichrist tries to enforce everyone to join him (Rev. 13:16).

Revelation 14

The 144,000 redeemed Jews evangelize the world and are protected by God. Revelation 14:8 announces that Babylon the Great has fallen because it made all the world commit spiritual adultery. Chapter 14 tells of the reaping of the harvest of the earth—the rapture of the church. Then there is another harvest, the "reaping of the vine of the earth," to be thrown into the winepress of the wrath of God. This speaks of the battle of Armageddon.

Revelation 15

This chapter introduces the seven angels having the seven last plagues. It states that these plagues "are filled up the wrath of God."

Revelation 16

Chapter 16 introduces Armageddon and the judgment of the false religious system called Mystery Babylon. God so hates false religion that He spends chapters 17 and 18 on the judgment of "the great whore." God always uses a woman to symbolize a church. He uses a virgin to symbolize His true church, and a harlot to symbolize the false, compromised church of the end-time.

Revelation 17–18

Revelation 17-18 describes the four kingdoms that will exist when the kingdom of God comes. They are depicted as animals and may be Great Britain, Germany, Russia, and the European Union, which seems to consist of ten nations (Rev. 17:12). No Islamic nations are mentioned. The little horn that arises is the antichrist, who conquers three kings, leaving eight. This little horn makes war with the saints and prevails (Dan. 2:44, 7:4–7, 7:20-21; Rev. 13:6–7).

Note: As of June 22, 2016, there are twenty-eight countries within the European Union. They include Austria, Belgium, Bulgaria, Croatia, the Republic of Cyprus, Czech Republic, Denmark, Estonia, Finland, France, Germany, Greece, Hungary, Ireland, Italy, Latvia, Lithuania, Luxembourg, Malta, the Netherlands, Poland, Portugal, Romania, Slovakia, Slovenia, Spain, and Sweden.

Revelation 18:4 tells us what to do to avoid the judgment of the nations: come out of her (this one-world government).

An underground church may exist during this time that does great exploits (Dan 11:32).

Revelation 19

God proceeds to describe His marriage to the true church. "Let us be glad and rejoice, and give honor to him: for the marriage of the Lamb is come, and his wife hath made herself ready." After the marriage, Jesus proceeds to the earth with His saints to fight the battle of Armageddon and to set up His kingdom.

Revelation 20

Revelation 20 describes events after Armageddon. Satan is bound for the next one thousand years. Jesus reigns on earth with His saints and those who are alive after Armageddon. Many are saved. After the thousand-year period has ended, Satan will be released to deceive the nations again. Satan is finally cast into the lake of fire, to be tormented forever. The books are opened for the final judgment, and all are judged according to their deeds (Rev. 20:12). Those whose names are not found written in the Lamb's Book of Life are cast into the lake of fire, where Satan and his angels are in eternal torment. The only way to get your name in the Lamb's Book of Life is to be born again, as described in Acts 2:38 and John 3, "Then Peter said unto them, Repent, and be baptized every one of you in the name of Jesus Christ for the remission of sins, and ye shall receive the gift of the Holy Ghost."

Revelation 21

In Revelation 21, John states that after the one-thousand-year millennium, there will be a new renovated heaven and earth. He is told that the new Jerusalem will be the capital city. The new Jerusalem is then described in great detail.

Revelation 22

The last chapter summarizes the goal of the entire book of Revelation. It describes the river of life and the tree of life that will be in the new Jerusalem. It also states that those who hear the sayings of the book of Revelation will be blessed. A dual warning is given. If any person adds to the things written in the book of Revelation, God will add to that person the plagues that are written in the book. If anyone takes away from the book of Revelation, God will take away his name from the Book of Life. Finally, in this concluding chapter, God emphasizes the central message of the book by saying three times, "Behold, I come quickly."

Judah ben Samuel's Prophecy

Please find below a link to Judah ben Samuel's prophecy about Jerusalem made in the year 1217, which has come true so far. It covers ten jubilee periods, or five hundred years, and predicts the return of Jerusalem to the Jews. This happened in the 2017 Jubilee (Hebrew year 5777) when the British general Allenby took Jerusalem from the Ottoman Turks without a shot fired by dropping leaflets from a newly invented mechanical flying machine called an airplane. On the following Jubilee in 1967 (The Seven-Day War), much land was annexed to Israel.

Link: http://destination-yisrael.biblesearchers.com/destination-yisrael/2012/12/rabbi-judah-ben-samuels-jubilee-prophecy-gives-the-year-of-the-messiah.html

The Bereshit Prophecy

The first word in the Bible, "In the beginning," is pronounced "Beresheet" in Hebrew and is encoded with several Hebrew words nested within it that tell a story about a Son who is a prince and creator that leaves His home to accomplish a planned work on the earth that results in the end of one thing (sin) and a beginning of another (eternity). The last letter in Bereshit is the Tav, which is shaped like a cross. In English, it is a *T*. Does this story sound familiar? Each letter of the Hebrew alphabet not only has a pictogram meaning but also a number value similar to Roman numerals. The last two letters in *Bereshit* may point to the time when Jesus would accomplish this work and go to the cross. The Tav has a number value of 400, and the Yod has a number value of 10, and when multiplied together is 4,000. As discussed, in the creation chapter, the earth was formed in 4004 BC according to Roman and Jewish history. Jesus was born about 4 BC, and Jesus was thirty-three and a half years old when He went to the cross. Some scholars believe Adam sinned at age thirty-three and a half years old. Doing the math shows that the work Jesus did on the cross was accomplished four thousand years after the earth was formed. I don't believe in coincidence when it comes to the Bible. There is much more to this prophecy that shows future events and timing that will amaze those that study it further.

Where Are We Now in the Prophecy?

The disciples ask Jesus about when the end of the age will happen and what signs will be there (Matt. 24:3; Luke 21:7; Mark 13:3).

The Treaty

A Mideast peace treaty is signed (Dan. 9:27; Matt. 24:15; 2 Thess. 2:1–4) and may trigger the start of the last seven years of tribulation. In August 2020, a peace treaty was signed between Israel and UAE that may be the start of this covenant.

The Catching Away of the Saints

The saints are removed from the earth and are caught up to meet Jesus in the air (1 Thess. 4:17; 1 Cor. 15:51–55; Matt. 24:41–42). Hopefully, before the tribulation starts.

The Temple

There is a Jewish temple and sacrifices at the end-time that hasn't been built yet. Jesus said the abomination of desolation occurs in the temple in the middle of the last seven years before Jesus Christ returns (Matt. 24:15; Dan. 9:27; 2 Thess. 2:4).

The Two Witnesses

The two witnesses begin their ministry (Rev. 11) about the middle of the last seven years.

The Antichrist Revealed

About the middle of the last seven years, the antichrist is revealed to the world (2 Thess. 2:3; Dan. 9:27). Satan is cast out of heaven and now knows his time is short. The Mideast peace treaty is broken, and Jesus warns those living in Judea to flee to the hills to avoid being killed.

Chapter Summary

One-third of the Bible contains prophecy. Many of the prophecies have been fulfilled with great accuracy. In this chapter we have examined prophecy in Daniel, Matthew, and Revelation to discover a shadow of future events for the purpose of showing God's plans before they happen. This reveals the omnipotent God, who has control over time and space. It also validates the scriptures that they are from God. Most prophecy revolves around Israel, the redeeming of mankind, and the world's Savior, Jesus Christ.

Book Summary

Like a puzzle with many pieces, we examined some of the biblical truth of who God is by looking at His various names, attributes, and creation. We looked at how mankind is made in three parts: a body to relate to our worldly realm, a spirit to relate to God, and a soul to relate to one another. We looked at God's creation as intricate artwork that reflects the artist's greatness. We examined some of the processes and plans that God has for each of us necessary to prepare us for eternal abundant life in God's heavenly kingdom.

We examined God's instructions on how mankind is to function. We investigated tools and gifts He has provided here and now that lead us to spiritual growth. We studied fulfilled prophecy and prophecy of future events to gain trust and understand God's redemption plans. There are many great promises in our future for new enhanced bodies that will not age, a new city, a new earth, and heaven, where we will dwell. Hopefully, we glimpsed eternity through examining dimensions and what Jesus told His disciples about the kingdom of God. I hope this perspective has expanded your understanding of reality from God's point of view.

> *But as it is written, Eye hath not seen, nor ear heard, neither have entered into the heart of man, the things which God hath prepared for them that love him. (1 Cor. 2:9 KJV)*

CPSIA information can be obtained
at www.ICGtesting.com
Printed in the USA
BVHW070932090221
599618BV00001B/48